Crafting Jewish

Fun holiday crafts and party ideas for the whole family

By **Rivky Koenig**
Photography by Jennifer Levy

Published by ARTSCROLL / SHAAR PRESS
4401 Second Avenue / Brooklyn, NY 11232 / (718) 921-9000
www.artscroll.com • www.craftingjewish.com

Distributed in Israel by SIFRIATI / A. GITLER
6 Hayarkon Street / Bnei Brak 51127 / Israel

Distributed in Europe by LEHMANNS
Unit E, Viking Business Park, Rolling Mill Road
Jarrow, Tyne and Wear, NE32 3DP / England

Distributed in Australia and New Zealand by GOLDS WORLD OF JUDAICA
3-13 William Street / Balaclava, Melbourne 3183, Victoria / Australia

Distributed in South Africa by KOLLEL BOOKSHOP
Ivy Common / 105 William Road/ Norwood 2192 / Johannesburg, South Africa

ISBN-10: 1-42260-817-4 / ISBN-13: 978-1-4226-0817-3

Printed in the USA by Noble Book Press

I am deeply grateful to all those people who have taught, helped, inspired and encouraged me from when I began crafting — my parents, in-laws, grandparents, and siblings. Most of all, to my husband and our children — you cheer on my every endeavor; I dedicate this book to you.

A special thank-you to Rabbi Meir Zlotowitz and the ArtScroll team for taking on this project with such enthusiasm. Thanks to Gedaliah Zlotowitz for guiding *Crafting Jewish* expertly through the nitty gritty of the publishing process, and Tzini Fruchthandler, indefatigable graphic designer and friend, for her extraordinary design work as well as her patience. Heartfelt thanks to my incredible editors, Felice Eisner and Judi Dick. This book wouldn't be the same without you. The incomparable ArtScroll staff worked tirelessly to make this book a success; thank you, Aviva Whiteman, Tova Ovits, Miriam Zakon, Eli Kroen, Gavriel Sanders, and Avrohom Biderman.

While you can't judge a book by its cover, this one is certainly beautiful. Photographer Jennifer Levy's unerring eye and exquisite photos truly make this book a work of art. It was exciting to work alongside her and her fabulous crew: Harry Pocius, Drake Patton, and Eric Vogel. Food and party stylist Susan Ottaviano and Ceci Loebl and Julie Hopper, her assistants, made every dish look delectable. Their low-key, friendly manner enhanced the experience. Special thanks to the cute kids in the photos.

Crafting Jewish would not have become reality without my experience developing and directing crafting projects. For this I owe thanks to Rabbi Yehuda and Mrs. Rasie Levi of Camp Hedvah for giving me the opportunity to work in a wonderful environment. Thanks to Perri Freund and Tziporah Schuck, as well as to all the staff and campers at Camp Hedvah for their unflagging enthusiasm for this project.

Friends old and new assisted me by reading the manuscript, lending props, or providing a listening ear. Among others, a heartfelt thank-you to Sara Hertzberg, Chumie Drillick, Hadassa Svei, Gitty Lowinger, and Chavie Leiner.

Most importantly, I cannot thank Hashem enough for giving me health, family, and everything I need, as well as this opportunity to share with others my experiences enhancing the special moments throughout the Jewish year.

A crafting note to adults

Crafting Jewish actively fosters and nurtures creativity and family fun. All the projects in this book have been chosen with care so that everyone in the family, from young children to teens and adults, can individually or collaboratively create something to make the holidays — or any day — special.

You will be introduced to a variety of crafting techniques, such as decoupage, stamping, beading, painting, antiquing, and more. Even if the last time you crafted was back in preschool, we encourage you to craft along with the kids and try your hand at a project yourself. Crafting is not an exact science — it's a wonderful medium for kids and adults to use their imagination, experiment, and have fun!

With this goal in mind, all the crafts and recipes in the book are written in a clear format and include a complete supply list, plus easy-to-follow step-by-step directions. Most of the supplies utilized for these crafts can be easily purchased at your local craft or hobby store; we list shops and websites where you can purchase those supplies that are not easily identifiable or that may be slightly harder to find. Although we may state a preference for a certain company's products, feel free to use a comparable brand.

A crafting note to kids

We know you're excited to make some fabulous projects and can't wait to start crafting, but before you pick up that paint brush or take out a mixing bowl, there are some preparations involved and a couple of things to keep in mind.

● **Get permission:** Always ask an adult before you use tools, glues, paints, cooking/baking supplies, or anything of value. Also have them make sure that the project you want to tackle is age-appropriate.

● **Check it out:** Before you start a project, check through the supply list to make sure you have everything you need (or a good substitute).

● **Read directions:** Take the time to read through each step carefully before you begin. It's important to know how much time you will need or if there is drying time involved.

● **Keep it clean:** Many projects can be messy, so you should prepare your crafting area ahead of time. Before painting or gluing, cover your work surface with newspapers. Keep a glass jar or mug of water nearby to put dirty brushes in so that they don't dry out and harden while you work.

● **A cut above:** When using a craft knife, place a self-healing mat (a large mat found at most craft stores) or a large piece of cardboard (you can cut one from a corrugated box) onto the crafting surface. Without this protection, you may cut through a countertop or table — not a good idea!

● **Measure twice, cut once:** This old saying is still good advice. Be sure your measurements are correct before cutting or adding ingredients to a recipe. This will help you avoid wasting supplies and doing unnecessary work.

- **Cover up:** Always wear a smock, apron, or old shirt when painting or working in the kitchen. Remember, if acrylic or fabric paint spills on your clothes, the stains won't come out.

- **Watch what you're doing:** Many of the tools used in these projects are sharp and must be used in a particular way. Be extra-cautious when using sharp tools, knives, and/or cutting devices. Read the instructions or manuals that come with the tools before using.

- **Clean up after yourself:** The best way to ensure that you will have other crafting opportunities is to put away all your supplies when you are done. Wipe down counters or tables with a wet washcloth or paper towels. If you are using paint brushes, wash them well to remove all the paint, and then let them air dry before storing them. After cooking or baking, wash all implements, dry them, and put them — as well as all remaining ingredients — back where they belong.

- **Save your scraps:** Keep a box filled with interesting scraps of paper, ribbon, or other materials that you find. You never know what might be the perfect finishing touch for a project, and, after using some of these items, you'll never look at "junk" in the same way.

- **Get creative and have fun:** Use the instructions as a guideline for the basic project, but you certainly could (rather, *should*) make the project your own by embellishing and decorating it according to your taste.

The kosher kitchen

Kosher cooks today have advantages undreamed of by their grandmothers: meat and poultry come from the butcher already koshered, and thousands of food products now have reliable rabbinic supervision — and the number is constantly growing!

Below is a summary of rules for kosher cooking. If your kitchen and appliances aren't yet kosher, or if you have kosher-cooking questions, contact a qualified rabbi for guidance.

- Meat and dairy are cooked and eaten separately, using separate utensils, including dishes and flatware. The utensils are also washed separately.
- All meat must be slaughtered by trained, certified kosher slaughterers; the blood is then removed in accordance with Jewish law. In many places, the butcher "koshers" the meat (removes the blood) using the prescribed salting and soaking process. If you need to "kosher" your own meat, consult a rabbi (in advance) about the proper procedure.
- Foods that are neither meat nor dairy (such as vegetables, eggs, grains) are called parve. They may be eaten with meat or dairy, but to retain their parve status they must be cooked in designated parve utensils.
- Fish with both fins and scales are kosher and do not require special koshering. All other seafood is prohibited. Fish is parve, but it may not be eaten together with meat.
- Eggs with bloodspots are discarded.
- All processed food products, including wine and cheese, require kosher certification.
- Produce must be washed well and checked for insects.
- Passover requires designated utensils and specially certified foods.

While these rules may sound complicated, they are not difficult to follow once your kitchen is set up correctly. Meat, dairy, and parve dishes and utensils are differentiated (often by color coding). A rabbi's phone number is kept handy for consultation if a mistake occurs. And the cook knows that both family and guests are eating food prepared in accordance with Jewish law, ensuring their spiritual, as well as physical, well being.

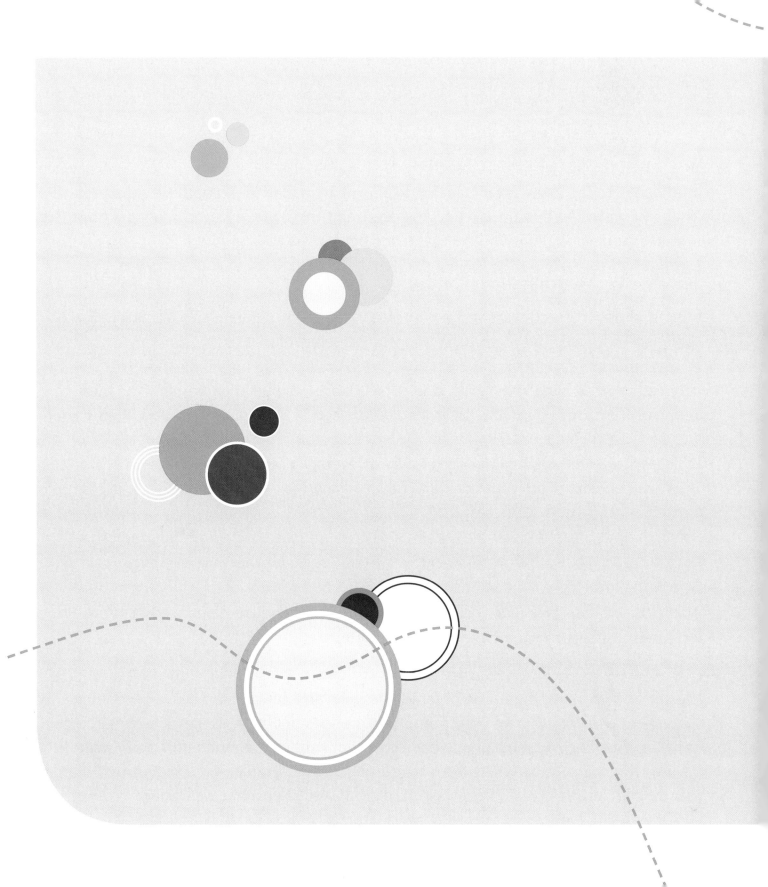

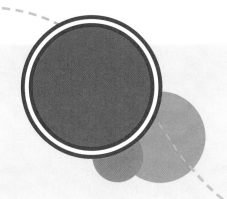

CONTENTS

Product Guide: Fun Crafting Stuff

① POMPOMS: balls of fiber, yarn, or ribbon to be glued to clothing, fabric, and craft projects.

② GLASS and CERAMIC PAINT: acrylic paints specially formulated for glass and ceramic surfaces. Follow manufacturer's specific instructions for application and drying. We use Folk Art Enamels by Plaid.

③ ACRYLIC CRAFT PAINT: water-based permanent paint in a variety of colors; used for painting wood and other surfaces including fabric. We use either the 2-ounce or 8-ounce Apple Barrel by Plaid.

④ OVEN BAKE CLAY: polymer modeling clay in assorted colors; it doesn't dry out after long exposure to air and can be painted with acrylic paint once baked. We use Sculpey brand clay.

⑤ CARDSTOCK LETTERS and TAGS: scrapbooking embellishments that add flair to scrapbooking, card-making, and paper crafting projects.

⑥ CARDSTOCK: thick crafting paper in assorted sizes, weights, colors, and patterns; it will not buckle or rip when embellishments are added.

⑦ WOODEN DOWEL: 12"-18" long rounded wood sticks used as flag handles and in other projects.

⑧ SEA GLASS: shards of glass that have been tumbled smooth by ocean water and sand or by machine; used in glass art, mosaics, and jewelry-making.

⑨ PAINTBRUSHES: brushes used to apply paint to a surface. Flat 1"-2" craft brushes are used to cover large surfaces. Short, fine point, or rounded bristle brushes are used for detail work.

⑩ COBBLETS: small smoothed shards of sea glass, sold in Michael's stores.

⑪ MICRO BEADS: teeny tiny beads used with double-sided adhesive tape.

⑫ PIPE CLEANERS: also called chenille stems; bendable bristle-covered wires used in many kids' craft projects.

⑬ FLAT GLASS MARBLES: glass marbles with one flat side and one rounded side.

⑭ RHINESTONES: crystal or plastic "gems" to decorate crafts or apparel. Adhere with various glues, depending on the material being used.

⑮ DIMENSIONAL FABRIC PAINT: specifically formulated for fabric; will not wash out. Sold in 1-ounce bottles with needle-nose applicator tip.

⑯ STAMP PAD: ink- or dye-covered pad used for rubberstamping images or inking edges of paper craft projects to create a distressed or aged look.

⑰ FOAM BRUSH: disposable flexible foam brush used to apply acrylic paint, wood stain, varnish, and decoupage medium to craft and wood projects.

⑱ MARKER: for paper crafting projects; use fine-tip markers for thin lines and details; use medium- or broad-tip markers for lettering/filling in outlines.

⑲ PAINT MARKER: permanent enamel-filled marker for writing on glass, ceramic, and plastic surfaces.

⑳ GEL PEN: roller ball pen filled with gel ink comes in many colors and in glitter, milky, and metallic versions for writing on dark paper or cardstock.

㉑ GLITTER: metallic plastic or glass bits in varying textures add pizzazz. Use with white glue, glittering glue, or double-sided tape or sheets.

㉒ RIBBON: lengths of fabric for decorating, tying gifts, hair accessories, and more, in many widths from ⅛", in satin, velvet, grosgrain, cotton, etc.

㉓ TRIM: decorative fabric accents, used on fabric and in decorating projects. Includes fringe, bullion trim, tassels, braid, etc.

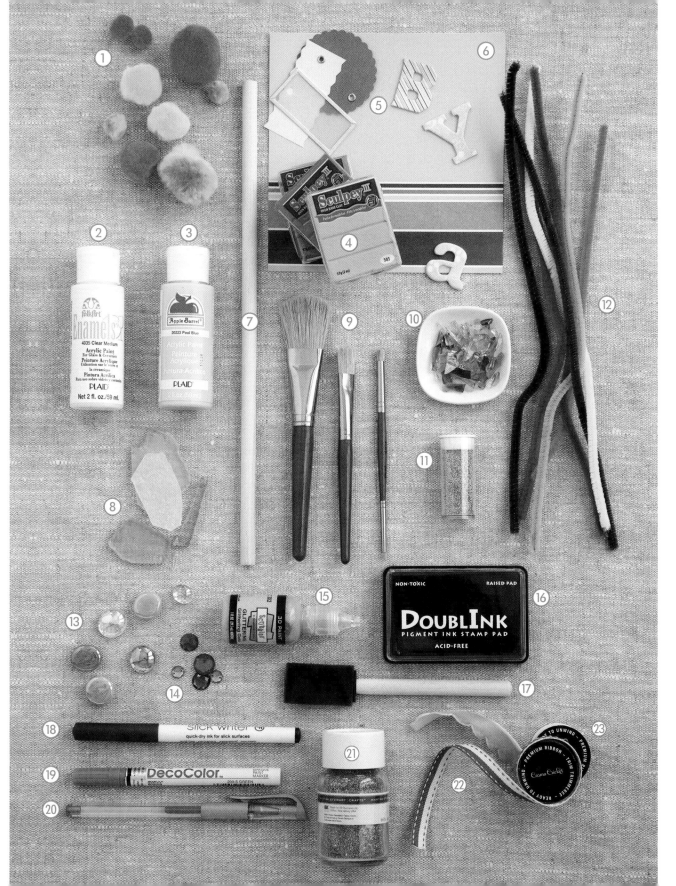

Cut It Up: Tools You Can Use

1. HOLE PUNCHER: basic metal office tool used to punch holes in paper for fastening or lacing items together.

2. UTILITY KNIFE (X-ACTO KNIFE): sharp knife with removable blades for precision cutting.

3. METAL WIRE: used for beading and other craft purposes; the higher the gauge number, the thinner the wire.

4. WIRE CUTTER: diagonal pliers used for cutting metal wire by making an indentation in the wire and forcing it apart, resulting in a smooth cut.

5. SANDPAPER: paper or other fiber coated with an abrasive material; used for smoothing out wood surfaces and for distressing papercrafting projects.

6. EYELETS and BRADS: small metal paper crafting embellishments that can be used to join two papers together or to reinforce a hole punched into paper or other materials. A hole must be punched in the crafting material before an eyelet or brad is inserted.

7. PORTABLE PAPER TRIMMER: paper-cutting device used to cut paper up to 12"x12" in straight lines; can usually cut a few sheets of paper or cardstock at a time. We use Fiskars Portable Paper Trimmer.

8. DECORATIVE-EDGE SCISSORS: scissors with blades that cut patterns into paper, similar to pinking shears, with a variety of designs to choose from. We are partial to Provo Craft Paper Shapers.

9. PINKING SHEARS: scissors with a sawtooth blade, primarily used for cutting fabric. The scissors create a zigzag edge which minimizes fraying.

10. CRAFT PUNCHES: tool designed to punch out die-cut paper shapes. Paper is placed in the craft punch opening and then a lever or button is pressed to punch down the metal die, forming a die-cut image. Craft punches come in a huge variety of shapes, sizes, and designs.

11. TAPE MEASURE: a flexible ruler made from cloth, plastic, or metal; a must for measuring fabric or objects that don't lie flat.

12. CROP-A-DILE: manufactured by We R Memory Keepers, this essential tool is an eyelet, snap, and grommet setter, as well as a $\frac{1}{8}$th and $\frac{3}{8}$th hole puncher. It punches through paper, cardstock, leather, and thin metal.

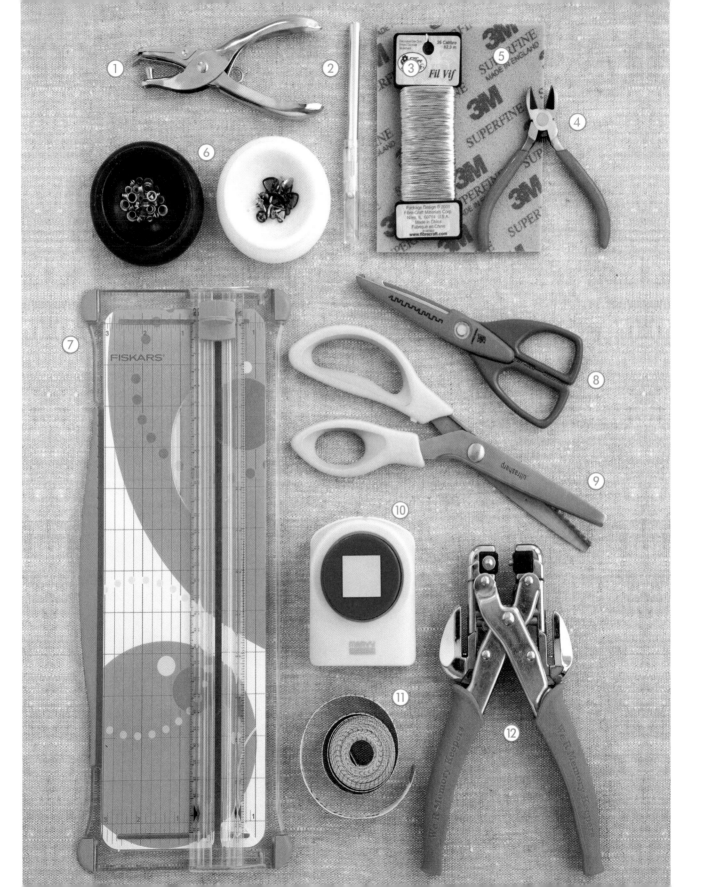

Stick It Together: Glues and Adhesives

① GLITTERING GLUE: glue specially formulated to adhere glitter, micro glitter or micro beads; in most cases white glue can be substituted. We like the Martha Stewart Crafts Glittering Glue.

② DOUBLE-SIDED ADHESIVE TAPE: dry adhesive for sticking together items such as paper, chipboard, photos, and light embellishments; it can be cut to exact size and is not visible in the completed project. American Crafts tape rolls come in assorted widths for different crafting needs.

③ DOUBLE-SIDED RED LINER TAPE: remarkable tape used to adhere beads, glitter, and other small items to wood, metal, and glass. The bond strengthens over time. We recommend using Provo Craft Art Accentz Terrifically Tacky Tape or sheets.

④ GLUE/TAPE RUNNER: dispensers that are rolled along to adhere papers, achieving a nice smooth finish. Many come with a refill option. They vary in bonding strength; some are repositionable. We like the Herma Dotto.

⑤ GLUE GUN and GLUE STICKS: heat-activated glue device; glue sticks are inserted into the gun. They create a strong bond on materials including wood and fabric. We use a low-temperature or dual-temperature glue gun.

⑥ STRAIGHT PINS: pins with rounded heads, used to hold fabric and/or trim together temporarily.

⑦ CRAFT GLUE: thick glue that dries clear, is flexible, and can be used on paper, wood, felt, etc., where a strong wet glue is needed. Aleene's Tacky Glue is the original and is our brand of choice.

⑧ FABRIC GLUE: strong, machine-washable glue that adheres fabric to fabric, lace, trims, sequins, buttons, rhinestones, and other embellishments. We recommend Aleene's OK to Wash It or FabriTac.

⑨ GLUE STICK: basic dry adhesive for adhering paper to paper.

⑩ WHITE GLUE: basic wet glue for simple crafting, it also can be thinned with a little water and used as a decoupage medium.

⑪ SELF-ADHESIVE TABS: dispensers that are rolled along to adhere photos or papers without a mess, achieving a nice smooth finish. Many come with a refill option. Check the package before purchasing, since they vary from light to ultra strong bonding strength; some are repositionable. We like the Herma Vario.

⑫ GLASS ETCHING CREAM: used to etch glass surfaces. We use Armour Etch.

⑬ DECOUPAGE MEDIUM: adhesive specifically formulated for decoupage projects. We always use Mod Podge; it comes in matte, gloss, and sparkle formulas. We use gloss unless otherwise specified.

⑭ MAGNETS: use to temporarily attach items to magnetic metal surfaces.

⑮ PUSHPINS: for affixing paper or cardboard to wood, cork, or drywall for display; can be removed easily.

⑯ DOUBLE-SIDED ADHESIVE FOAM DOTS and SQUARES: used to add dimension to a paper crafting project. Your adhered item will pop up from the surface. We use EK Success 3-D Dots in white or black.

⑰ PERMANENT BONDING ADHESIVE: extremely strong glue used to adhere glass to glass as well as to metals, ceramics, stone, wood, and some plastics. It emits a strong odor — use in a well-ventilated area and read all instructions and warnings before use. E6000 is our brand of choice.

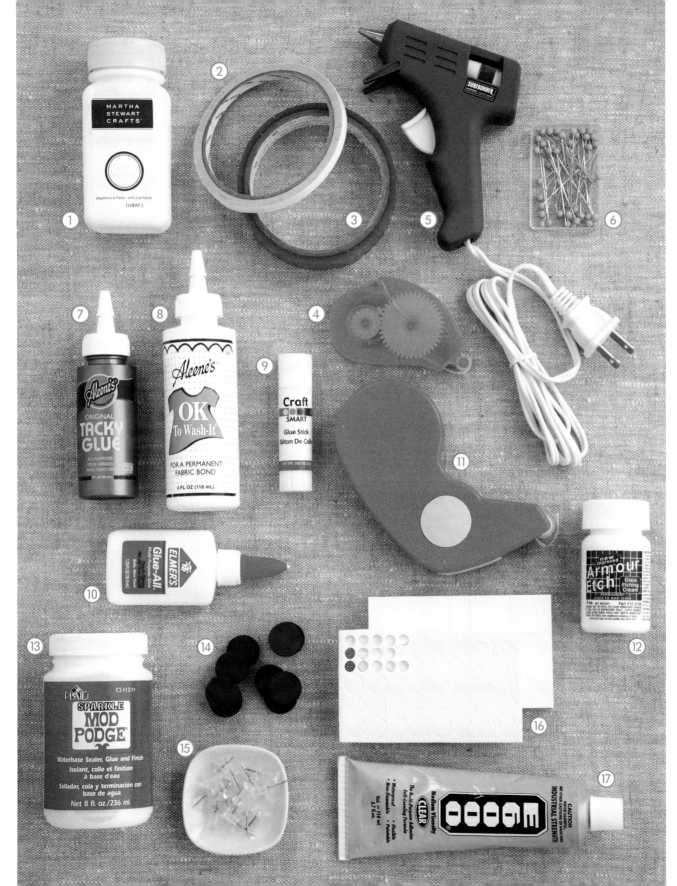

Cook Up Some Fun: Basic Kitchen Tools and Gadgets

① FOOD PROCESSOR: used to mix, chop, purée, and shred foods with ease.

② MEASURING CUPS: used to measure dry ingredients. Scoop dry ingredients into the measuring cup of choice, then level off excess with knife for perfect measurements.

③ MICROPLANE GRATER/ZESTER: used to finely grate or shave ingredients such as cheese, chocolate, ginger, and other firm ingredients. Use it to remove the zest of lemon and oranges.

④ MEASURING SPOONS: used to measure small amounts of ingredients.

⑤ SILICONE BASTING AND PASTRY BRUSH: perfect for brushing egg onto pastry or dough; it also can be used to baste hot chicken or meat. Heat safe to over 500°F.

⑥ CHEF'S KNIFE: a sharp knife that is a must for almost all cutting and chopping tasks.

⑦ SLOTTED SPOON: a spoon with slots, holes, or other openings (such as our spoon's smiley face) that allow liquid to drain out while holding the solid food in the bowl of the spoon.

⑧ ROLLING PIN: used to roll dough flat for pastries, cookies, and some yeast doughs.

⑨ WHISK: a tool used for mixing a liquid mixture smooth, or to incorporate air into a mixture.

⑩ IMMERSION BLENDER: great for blending food smooth in the container in which it is being prepared. No need to get an extra bowl or blender dirty.

⑪ SILICONE SPATULA: perfect for mixing wet and dry ingredients together, as well as for scraping down a mixing bowl. The silicone spatula has the added benefit of being heatproof to high temperatures so you can use it for removing hot food from frying pans — and it also won't scratch cookware!

ROSH HASHANAH

Rosh Hashanah. The Jewish new year. The holiday brings to mind fresh starts and new beginnings — an auspicious time to reflect on the year that has passed and to request a sweet year to come. It is a time to pray and to listen to the sound of the shofar, the ram's horn that is blown to awaken the spirit of repentance, to proclaim that God is our king, and to re-establish our connection with Him.

While the awe-inspiring days of Rosh Hashanah are in essence a time for reflection and repentance, it is also a happy holiday filled with hope and optimism. Particularly, it is a time for people to reconnect with one another, and to reach out to family, friends, and to whomever needs us.

A beautiful way to demonstrate that we care about them is by utilizing our creativity and sending those to whom we are close something we've made with our own hands. Whether it is a stunning decoupaged dish for the apples and honey, a sweet handcrafted shanah tova card with good wishes for the new year, or a yummy carrot cake in a personalized package, this is the time for giving to others as we wish them — and ourselves — a happy, sweet new year.

Apples are a seasonal fall crop and are in great abundance around Rosh Hashanah.

Try this project using a variety of apples. The different types and sizes of apples will create a beautiful assortment of stamped images. Don't limit your stamping to cards — the apples can be stamped onto paper bags, cloth or paper napkins, or even a fabric tablecloth.

apple-stamped card

What you will need:

- ☐ knife
- ☐ apple
- ☐ paper towel
- ☐ red acrylic paint
- ☐ paper plate
- ☐ package of 20 blank cards
- ☐ metallic markers

How to do it:

1. Carefully cut the apple in half from top to bottom (try to leave the stem intact while cutting). Blot the cut sides on paper towel so that the apple halves will be as dry as possible.

2. Squirt or pour a small amount of paint onto the paper plate.

3. Dip the cut side of the apple into paint, taking care to completely cover the dipped side with paint.

5. Stamp the apple onto the card and carefully lift the apple so that the apple stamp does not smudge. Repeat dipping the same apple half in paint, stamping as many times as necessary. Allow to dry.

6. Use metallic markers to write *Shanah Tova* on the card.

7. Repeat for remaining cards.

Estimated time: 30 minutes
Drying Time: 30 minutes

Crafting Shanah Tova cards is a great way to get creative with scrapbooking supplies. I like to take blank cards and decorate them with scraps of paper, stickers, tags, ribbons, and markers. I usually use a pack of scrapbooking paper with its embellishments because then all the coordinating papers and accessories are in one place, and I don't have to think about matching colors and styles.

shanah tova cards

What you will need:

- ☐ package of 20 blank cards
- ☐ scrapbooking paper and embellishment pack
- ☐ pencil and ruler
- ☐ scissors and/or paper cutter
- ☐ glue stick or glue runner
- ☐ glue lines or dots
- ☐ double-sided adhesive foam dots
- ☐ embellishment options: ribbons, rickrack, buttons, flowers, tags, stickers
- ☐ alphabet stickers or markers

How to do it:

1. For each card, place the front of the card onto the back of a piece of scrapbook paper. Trace the card and cut the shape out of the scrapbook paper (you can also cut out a rectangle of scrapbook paper that is slightly smaller than the card).

2. Use the glue stick or glue runner to adhere the rectangle to the front of the card.

3. Attach ribbon, tags, and other embellishments of your choice to the front of the card, using glue lines or glue dots. If you want the embellishment to be raised, attach with foam dots.

4. Use alphabet stickers to spell out your message or use markers to write your message on the front of the card.

Variation:

1. Copy and cut out the apple, stem, and leaf templates (page 260).

2. Trace the shapes onto the back of patterned scrapbook paper. Cut out.

3. Use a glue stick to attach the apple, stem, and leaf to the front of a card covered in scrapbook paper.

Estimated time: 10 – 20 minutes per card

have a happy sweet
new year. Shanah Tova.

Shanah t

This collage is a great way to display the cards that have been sent to wish your family a Shanah Tova. If you don't have enough pictures, or if you want to use a specific image, you can download clip art or add some of your own drawings. To protect the collage from moisture, cover it with clear contact paper or laminate it at your local copy shop. This collage can be used as a place mat or picture; display it on an outside door by threading ribbon into a bow at the top and hanging it from a nail or doorknob. It can also be hung in your succah as a beautiful decoration.

shanah tova card collage

What you will need:

- [ ] ruler and pencil
- [ ] posterboard
- [ ] scissors or paper cutter
- [ ] 1 (12"x12") sheet scrapbook paper
- [ ] decorative-edge scissors
- [ ] glue stick
- [ ] assorted cards or clip art
- [ ] clear contact paper, optional
- [ ] hole punch, optional
- [ ] ribbon, optional

How to do it:

1. Use your ruler and pencil to measure and outline a 12"x14" rectangle on the posterboard. Cut out the rectangle using scissors or a paper cutter.

2. Measure and outline a 10"x12" rectangle on the scrapbook paper. Use the decorative-edge scissors to cut out the scrapbook-paper rectangle.

3. Cut out the pictures from the cards, using either type of scissors. Arrange the images attractively on the scrapbook paper, overlapping them slightly. When you are satisfied with the layout, and working with one picture at a time, lift it, spread glue on its back, and replace it on the scrapbook paper.

4. Center the scrapbook paper on the posterboard so that there is a 1-inch border on all sides. Use the glue stick to glue the scrapbook paper to the posterboard.

5. If you are covering the collage with contact paper, measure the contact paper so that it is large enough to cover both sides of the collage. Apply the contact paper to the front and back of the collage, pulling away the backing of the contact paper slowly and smoothing it down as you apply it.

6. If you plan to hang the collage, punch a hole 3 inches from each top corner of the posterboard, 1 inch from the top edge. Thread the ribbon through the holes and tie a large bow (see photo).

Estimated time: 30 – 45 minutes

On Rosh Hashanah night we eat challah and an apple slice, each dipped in honey to symbolize our hope for a good, sweet new year. This apple-shaped honey server is decorated simply with the heartfelt sentiment.

painted honey dish

What you will need:

- ☐ masking tape
- ☐ apple-shaped glass dish (made by Libby), found in most housewares stores
- ☐ red fine-point paint marker
- ☐ gold fine-point paint marker
- ☐ wet paper towel, if needed

How to do it:

1. Tape a piece of masking tape evenly around the middle of the bowl. This will be a guide to keep the lettering in a straight line.

2. Use the red paint marker to write *Shanah Tova u'Metukah*, in either Hebrew or English, on the bowl above the tape. Parts of letters that extend below the tape should be added after the other letters dry and the tape is removed. If any of the letters smudge or are not written correctly, you can quickly rub off the mistake with a wet paper towel. Let dry, and then peel off the masking tape.

3. Outline and color in the leaves on the glass cover with the gold paint marker.

Note: Gently hand-wash only.

Estimated time: 30 minutes
Drying Time: 30 minutes

"Decoupage" is the French word for the art of decorating with paper cutouts varnished or lacquered onto a smooth surface. I usually cut designs from pretty napkins and/or wrapping paper for my decoupage projects. Here, the beautiful design shines through from under the face of the glass plate. It is a stunning way to present the apple for dipping on Rosh Hashanah night. This plate should be wiped clean with a damp paper towel — the back surface should not become wet.

decoupaged apple dish

What you will need:

- [ ] luncheon napkin or wrapping paper with pictures of apples and/or fruit
- [ ] 1 smooth-bottomed glass plate
- [ ] scissors
- [ ] decoupage medium, such as Mod Podge
- [ ] disposable plastic bowl
- [ ] 2 (1"-2"-wide) foam brushes
- [ ] white acrylic paint
- [ ] gold acrylic paint
- [ ] gold paint marker

How to do it:

1. Open the napkin and place it under the plate so that an overall design will be on the back of the plate. Decide which part of the design you want to affix to the plate. Cut out that section of the napkin, making sure that it is the size of the plate or slightly larger.

2. Turn the plate over.

3. Pour a small amount of Mod Podge into the plastic bowl. Dip a foam brush into the Mod Podge and smear a thin coat of it onto the back of the entire plate. Carefully center the napkin, face down, on the Mod Podge-covered surface and smooth out any air bubbles.

4. Use a foam brush to spread another thin coat of Mod Podge to cover the back of the entire napkin. It is okay if the napkin wrinkles slightly; if any rips occur, just smooth the ripped part together. Let dry for at least 1 hour.

5. Use your scissors to trim off any pieces of hardened napkin that extend over of the edge of the plate.

6. When the napkin is completely dry, use a foam brush to coat the back of the plate with white acrylic paint. Allow to dry completely. Paint over the white paint with a coat of gold paint. Allow to dry completely.

7. Use a gold paint marker to draw a thin line around the top edge of the plate.

Estimated time: 30 minutes – 1 hour
Total drying time: 3 – 5 hours, divided

On Rosh Hashanah night we eat foods that have symbolic meanings. *Siman* is the Hebrew word for "symbol." These foods and the *Yehi Ratzon* (literally, "May it be Your will") petition that we recite over them symbolize our desire for a good, healthy year. Each entreaty begins with the words, "May it be Your will (Hashem, our God and the God of our forefathers), that …."

Set out a sectioned tray or a large tray or platter that can hold an assortment of small dishes. Place the traditional siman in each section or plate. Insert a small flag inscribed with the appropriate ending to the *Yehi Ratzon* prayer, in either Hebrew or English, into the food item to which it applies.

siman markers

What you will need:

- [ ] ruler and pencil
- [ ] colored cardstock or heavy paper
- [ ] scissors and/or paper cutter
- [ ] white cardstock
- [ ] white glue
- [ ] skewers

How to do it:

1. For each flag, use a ruler and pencil to mark a 3½"x2" rectangle on the back of the colored cardstock. Use scissors or a paper cutter to cut out the rectangle.

2. Photocopy the *Yehi Ratzon* template (page 256-257) onto the white cardstock.

3. Cut out the *Yehi Ratzon* and glue it to the center of the colored rectangle. Place a small dab of glue on the side of the top 1" of a skewer and glue it to the back center of the cardstock rectangle. Let dry.

4. Repeat for the remaining *Yehi Ratzons*.

Estimated time: 10 minutes for each flag
Drying Time: 30 minutes

PRE-ROSH HASHANAH MAKE AND TAKE

Rosh Hashanah is a time of renewal and beginning — and what better way to prepare for the year than by crafting Shanah Tova cards and sending them along with some home-baked treats to relatives and friends. Better yet, how about baking and/or crafting cards for the elderly and/or sick. They will be delighted with your efforts, and you will have done a chessed (good deed) in advance of Rosh Hashanah.

Since Rosh Hashanah usually occurs in September when everyone is busy with the start of the school year, the ideal time to bake cakes for the holiday and to craft Shanah Tova cards is at the end of August, when camp programs have ended and school has not yet begun. The sole preparation for this get-together is to make sure that you have all the craft supplies and the recipe ingredients on hand. (It's no fun to be in midst of making a recipe together when you realize, "Uh oh, no sugar!")

While the cakes are baking (after cleaning up, of course), craft the cards with the prepared supplies. You will be thrilled to use your time in such a fun and productive manner — it sure beats looking into the oven window, watching the cakes bake ever so sloooowly.

■ Baking area set up:

First decide which cakes or cookies you will be baking. The honey cake (page 34), carrot cake (page 36), and rugelach (page 41) that we feature are all great options because they are easy to bake and package — they also freeze well.

Cover the counters with disposable tablecloths, so that there will be less mess to clean up when you're done. Prepare all recipe ingredients, baking supplies, and pans in one central location. Keep in mind that mini loaf pans are the perfect size for gift-giving. Copy the recipes onto cards so that everyone can follow along easily, and there will be no mix-ups! To be sure that you don't burn anything while crafting, set a kitchen timer to ring when the baking is done.

■ Crafting area set up:

While the cakes are baking, get to work on the cards. Prepare another area, preferably away from your main baking spot. Set out blank cards, scrapbooking paper, paper cutters and scissors, adhesives and all sorts of embellishments. Use our card-making instructions on pages 20-22 to inspire you. Have tissue paper, bags, bakery boxes, stickers, and tags on hand, as well, for packaging the baked goods when they have cooled.

■ Food:

Baking and crafting can certainly make you hungry. Prepare snacks such as pretzels, popcorn, and nuts and set them out in large bowls near your crafting area. Add pitchers of drinks, but don't place them on the crafting table, since you don't want spills to ruin your creative efforts. For a refreshing and timely treat, prepare the Pomegranate Punch (page 42) and Colorful Fruit Salad (page 44) and serve them as well.

.... perfect honey cake ....

What you will need:

- ☐ 3 mini loaf pans, 3 (8") round pans, or 1 tube pan
- ☐ baking spray
- ☐ measuring cups and spoons
- ☐ 2-cup liquid measuring cup
- ☐ electric mixer with large bowl
- ☐ large bowl
- ☐ spatula or spoon
- ☐ wire rack

Ingredients:

- ☐ 1 cup boiling water
- ☐ 1 tablespoon instant coffee
- ☐ 1 teaspoon baking soda
- ☐ 4 large eggs
- ☐ 1 cup white sugar
- ☐ ½ cup light-brown sugar
- ☐ ¾ cup oil
- ☐ 1 cup honey
- ☐ 1 tablespoon lemon juice
- ☐ 2½ cups flour
- ☐ 2 teaspoons baking powder
- ☐ 1 teaspoon cinnamon
- ☐ ¼ teaspoon ground ginger
- ☐ ¼ teaspoon ground nutmeg

I love this honey cake. It's rich and perfect for Rosh Hashanah morning and as a dessert.

How to do it:

1. Preheat oven to 325°F. Lightly spray the pan(s) with baking spray. Set aside.

2. Pour 1 cup boiling water into a 2-cup measuring cup. Add 1 tablespoon coffee and set aside to cool.

3. Dissolve the baking soda in the coffee (it will bubble a bit).

4. Place the eggs, white sugar, light-brown sugar, oil, honey, and lemon juice into the mixer bowl. Beat until the sugars are dissolved and the batter is thick and creamy, about 3 minutes.

5. Place the flour, baking powder, cinnamon, ginger, and nutmeg into a large bowl. Use a spatula or spoon to combine.

6. With the mixer on low speed, slowly add some of the flour mixture to the batter, then some coffee, some more flour mixture, the rest of the coffee, and the rest of the flour mixture.

7. When the batter is smooth (don't overbeat), pour it into the prepared pan(s), filling them ⅔-full, scraping batter from the sides of the bowl with the spatula.

8. Place pan(s) into the hot oven and bake for 1 hour or 1 hour and 15 minutes, depending on pan size used.

9. Remove from oven and cool in pan on a wire rack.

Estimated prep time: 15 minutes
Bake time: 1 hour for mini loaf pans and round pans;
 1 hour and 15 minutes for tube pan
Parve • Yield: one tube cake or three mini loaves or round cakes

one-bowl carrot cake

What you will need:

- ☐ 3 mini loaf pans
- ☐ baking spray
- ☐ can opener
- ☐ strainer
- ☐ 2 small bowls
- ☐ vegetable peeler
- ☐ grater or food processor
- ☐ 2 large mixing bowls
- ☐ measuring cups and spoons
- ☐ spoon and spatula
- ☐ toothpick
- ☐ wire rack

Carrot Cake Ingredients:

- ☐ 1 (8-ounce) can crushed pineapple
- ☐ 3 medium carrots
- ☐ 2¼ cups flour
- ☐ 2 teaspoons baking soda
- ☐ 2 teaspoons cinnamon
- ☐ ½ teaspoon salt
- ☐ 1¼ cup sugar
- ☐ 3 tablespoons oil
- ☐ 2 eggs
- ☐ 1 teaspoon vanilla extract

Frosting Ingredients:

- ☐ ½ cup dairy or nondairy cream cheese, softened
- ☐ 3 cups confectioners' sugar
- ☐ 1 teaspoon vanilla extract
- ☐ 1 tablespoon reserved pineapple liquid

This carrot cake is a moist, delicious treat. A great feature about it is the fact that all the ingredients are mixed in one bowl — making clean-up a snap!

Bake the cake in mini loaf pans so that you can share with neighbors and friends — it will be a sweet Rosh Hashanah treat.

How to do it:

1. Preheat oven to 350°F. Spray the pans with baking spray and set aside.

2. Open the can of pineapple. Use a strainer to drain the pineapple liquid into a small bowl. Reserve liquid.

3. Using the vegetable peeler and grater, peel the carrots and grate them into a bowl. You can also use a food processor fitted with the shredder or grater attachment. Add drained pineapple and 3 tablespoons of reserved pineapple liquid. Set aside.

4. In a large mixing bowl, combine the flour, baking soda, cinnamon, and salt. Stir with a spoon.

5. Add sugar, oil, eggs, and vanilla to the flour mixture. Stir with a spatula until batter is blended well. Add carrot-pineapple mixture and stir to blend.

6. Pour the batter into the prepared pans, filling them ⅔ full, and smooth the top with the spatula.

7. Place pans into the hot oven and bake for 30–35 minutes, or until a toothpick inserted into the center comes out clean. Remove from oven and place on a wire rack to cool.

8. Prepare the frosting: Using a spoon and small bowl, stir together cream cheese, confectioners' sugar, vanilla, and 1 tablespoon reserved pineapple liquid. Use a spatula to spread frosting on cooled cake.

Note: This recipe can also be baked in a 9"x13" pan for 45 minutes–1 hour.

Estimated prep time: 30 minutes
Bake time: 35 minutes (for mini loaf pans)
Cooling time: 1 hour
Frosting time: 10 minutes
Dairy or Parve • Yield: 3 mini loaves

·········· round raisin challah ··········

What you will need:

- [ ] measuring cups and spoons
- [ ] electric stand mixer, dough hook, bowl
- [ ] pastry brush
- [ ] plastic wrap
- [ ] dish towel
- [ ] pastry board
- [ ] knife
- [ ] 4 (8") and/or 6 (4") round baking pans
- [ ] small bowl
- [ ] fork

Ingredients:

- [ ] 4 cups lukewarm water
- [ ] 8 teaspoons dry yeast (or 2 ounces fresh yeast)
- [ ] 2 tablespoons sugar
- [ ] 4 eggs
- [ ] 1 cup vegetable oil plus 1 tablespoon oil, divided
- [ ] 1 cup sugar
- [ ] 2 tablespoons table salt
- [ ] 1 (5-pound) bag of flour plus more for sprinkling
- [ ] 1 cup raisins
- [ ] 1 egg, for eggwash

This challah recipe makes delicious sweet challah. Although it takes some effort, the yummy smell and taste of homemade challah are beyond compare. If you follow the directions carefully, you'll be rewarded with fabulous results. Omit the raisins and braid the dough following the instructions on page 226 for every Shabbat.

How to do it:

1. Pour the lukewarm water into the bowl of an electric mixer fitted with a dough hook. Add the yeast and 2 tablespoons sugar. Let the yeast stand for 10 minutes, or until it gets bubbly and frothy.

2. Add the eggs, oil, sugar, and salt to the yeast mixture. Stir on low until just combined.

3. With the mixer set on low, add flour, 1 cup at a time, to the mixer bowl. The dough will thicken and will become more difficult to mix with each additional cup.

4. Knead the dough on a medium setting for 5–10 minutes until smooth and elastic. If the dough is sticky, knead it a little longer. The dough is ready to rise when you poke your finger into it and the dough springs back toward you.

5. With the pastry brush, brush the top of the dough with the tablespoon of oil. Cover the bowl with plastic wrap and then cover that with a clean dish towel. Place the bowl in a warm spot and let rise until dough doubles in size.

6. When the dough has doubled in size, sprinkle flour on a pastry board or on a clean counter. Remove the towel and plastic wrap from the bowl and punch down the dough. Place the dough on the prepared board or counter. Remove a piece of dough for the mitzvah of *hafrashat challah* and say the blessing. (See page 40 for more details.)

7. Use the knife to cut dough into 4-6 equal pieces. Sprinkle with raisins. Roll each piece into a long strip with one end thicker than the other. For large challahs that fit into an 8" round pan, the dough strip should be about 18 inches long; for a 4" pan the strip should be about 10 inches long. Make sure to roll the raisins into the dough. Place the thicker end of each strip into the center of the round pan and wind the rest of the strip around that end. Tuck the narrower end under the challah. Repeat with each dough strip. Or, for braided challah (see photo), roll 3

pieces of dough into 15" strips. Braid the three strips together. With the braided challah on a flat surface, hold the top of the braid with one hand and use your other hand to wrap the braid around the center to form a braided circle. Tuck the end of the braid under and place the braided round challah into a pan.

8. Let the challahs rise in the pans for 30 minutes. Preheat oven to 350°F.

9. Beat the remaining egg well with a fork. Use the pastry brush to brush the beaten egg onto the challahs.

10. Place pans into the hot oven and bake for 45 minutes. Remove from oven to check for doneness by removing from pans and tapping the bottom. If they sound hollow and look dry, they are done. If not, replace in pans and bake additional 10–15 minutes. Remove from oven and let cool.

Total estimated prep time: 1 hour
Rise and shape time: 2 – 3½ hours
Bake time: 45 minutes
Parve • Yield: 6 small/medium challahs or 4 large challahs

Hafrashat Challah:

The mitzvah of challah addresses our relationship with the fundamental staff of life. In Judaism, the mundane process of baking bread is elevated to holiness by a ritual recalling days of ancient Jewish glory.

In the days of the Holy Temple in Jerusalem, the *Kohanim* were not apportioned farmland, for they were required to devote themselves entirely to the study of Torah and to the Temple service. Their relationship with the rest of the Jewish nation was defined by their role as spiritual mentors.

A system of tithes and gifts of food was mandated by the Torah for the support of the *Kohanim*. One of these gifts was "challah": Anyone who baked bread was required to give a portion of the dough to a *Kohen*. Taking the dough to the *Kohen* strengthened their mutual bond — kind words would be exchanged, family inquiries made, a lesson in Torah learned. One's link with those who serve God was reinforced.

Today, *Kohanim* are not permitted to accept the separated dough, yet the mitzvah of *hafrashat challah* remains. The obligation begins when kneading at least 2 lbs., 10 ounces of dough made from one or more of five grains: wheat, barley, oats, rye, or spelt. A piece of dough the size of an olive is removed and burned. (You can wrap it in foil and put it in the oven until it is too charred to be edible.) If the batch is larger (legal opinions of the minimum amount range from 3 lbs, 10.7 oz. to 4 lbs., 15.2 oz.), a blessing is made before removing the dough: Blessed are You, Hashem, our God, King of the universe, Who has sanctified us with His commandments and has commanded us to separate challah from the dough.

The name for our special Shabbat bread derives from the mitzvah associated with it. By sanctifying our loaves, we demonstrate that we appreciate God's blessings; and in keeping alive the practice of reserving this portion, we express our faith that someday the Jewish People will be able to return to the Temple and to the spiritual level that once was ours.

···· rugelach ····

What you will need:

- [ ] knife
- [ ] electric mixer
- [ ] measuring cups and spoons
- [ ] spatula
- [ ] 4 plastic food storage bags
- [ ] pastry board and rolling pin
- [ ] 9" dinner plate
- [ ] pizza cutter or sharp knife
- [ ] baking sheets
- [ ] parchment paper
- [ ] wire rack

Dough Ingredients:

- [ ] 2 sticks butter or margarine, softened
- [ ] ¼ cup confectioners' sugar
- [ ] 8 ounces nondairy whipping cream (dessert topping), such as Rich's Whip, not whipped
- [ ] 1 teaspoon vanilla extract
- [ ] 5½ cups flour

Filling Ingredients:

- [ ] oil, as needed
- [ ] 1 cup sugar and 1 tablespoon cinnamon, mixed together
- [ ] apricot jam and 1 cup ground walnuts
- [ ] ½ cup cocoa mixed with 1 cup sugar

Rugelach is Yiddish for "little twists." These pastries are spread with your choice of filling and rolled or twisted (see photo on page 32) to make a wonderful addition to your Rosh Hashanah menu.

How to do it:

1. Use the knife to cut the margarine into small chunks. Place the margarine into the mixer bowl and beat on medium-high until it is creamy. Add confectioners' sugar, whipping cream, and vanilla; mix till well combined.

2. Turn the mixer to a low setting and slowly add the flour. Increase the speed and mix until dough forms.

3. Evenly divide the dough into four pieces. Place each piece into a plastic bag and refrigerate for 4 hours or overnight. (You can also freeze the dough. Let it defrost for a few minutes before using.)

4. Preheat the oven to 350°F. Prepare the baking sheets by covering them with parchment paper. Set aside.

5. Sprinkle flour onto a clean counter or pastry board. Working with one piece of dough at a time, use the rolling pin to roll out a ¼"-thick circle. For a perfect circle, place a dinner plate over the dough circle and trim away dough that sticks out around the edge of the plate. Remove the plate and reroll the scraps with the next piece of dough.

6. For the cinnamon or cocoa filling, smear dough circle with 1 tablespoon of oil. Then sprinkle the dough with the filling, leaving a ½-inch border. For the jam-nut filling, smear the jam on the dough circle, leaving a ½-inch border. Sprinkle ground walnuts over the jam.

7. Use the pizza cutter or sharp knife to cut the circle into 12–16 triangles, the way you would cut a pizza pie. Roll each triangle from the wide end to the narrow point. Repeat with the remaining dough.

8. Place the rugelach, point side down, onto the prepared baking sheets.

9. Place baking sheets into the hot oven and bake for 30 minutes, or until the rugelach edges start to brown.

10. Remove sheets from oven; transfer rugelach onto a wire rack to cool.

Estimated prep time: 30 minutes per batch

Chill time: 4 hours or overnight

Bake time: 30 minutes

Dairy or Parve • Yield: 48–64 rugelach

•••••••• pomegranate syrup ••••••••

What you will need:

- [ ] liquid measuring cup
- [ ] small pot
- [ ] measuring cups and spoons
- [ ] spoon
- [ ] storage container, optional

Ingredients:

- [ ] 1 cup pomegranate juice, such as Pom Wonderful
- [ ] ¾ cup sugar
- [ ] 1 teaspoon lemon juice

The pomegranate is eaten on Rosh Hashanah because we want our mitzvot and good deeds to be as plentiful as the many, possibly 613, seeds in the pomegranate.

Turn pomegranate juice into a sparkly drink with this easy pomegranate syrup recipe. Use the remaining syrup on the Colorful Fruit Salad (page 44) or drizzle it over pancakes. Yum!

How to do it:

1. In a small pot, combine pomegranate juice and sugar.

2. Place the pot on the stove and turn the heat to medium. Stir the sugar and juice with the spoon. When the sugar is completely dissolved, lower the heat. Let the mixture simmer (there should be tiny bubbles in the pot) for 5 minutes, or until syrupy and sticky. Remove from heat.

3. Stir in lemon juice and let cool. Transfer the syrup to a storage container or use it in the following recipes.

Estimated prep time: 15 minutes
Parve • Yield: 1½ cups syrup

•••••••• pomegranate punch ••••••••

What you will need:

- [ ] pitcher
- [ ] long spoon
- [ ] liquid measuring cup
- [ ] sharp knife and cutting board

Ingredients:

- [ ] 1 cup pomegranate syrup
- [ ] ⅓ cup orange juice
- [ ] 3 cups seltzer
- [ ] orange or lemon

This refreshing drink is a cinch to make, tastes great, and is very healthful.

How to do it:

1. Pour the pomegranate syrup, orange juice, and seltzer into a pitcher. Mix the punch with the long spoon.

2. Wash the orange or lemon very well and dry it. On the cutting board, slice the orange or lemon into circles with the sharp knife. Cut each circle in half and float the slices in the punch. Serve immediately so that seltzer does not go flat.

Estimated prep time: 10 minutes
Parve • Yield: 4 – 5 cups

········ colorful fruit salad ········

What you will need:

- ☐ vegetable peeler
- ☐ sharp knife
- ☐ cutting board
- ☐ spoon
- ☐ large bowl
- ☐ dessert bowls or compote dishes

Ingredients:

- ☐ assorted fruits: honeydew, cantaloupe, pineapple, kiwis, mangoes, strawberries, figs, grapes, star fruits, prickly pears (sabras)
- ☐ 1 cup pomegranate arils
- ☐ 1 cup pomegranate syrup

It's customary to eat fruits you haven't eaten all year on the second night of Rosh Hashanah so that you can recite the shehecheyanu blessing. This fruit salad can be made with an assortment of fruits and melons. Those listed are just a suggestion. Try to include fruit(s) from the 7 species of fruit native to the Land of Israel, such as figs, dates, grapes, and pomegranates. The pomegranate syrup adds a delightful taste to any fruit assortment.

How to do it:

1. Wash the fruit well. Use the vegetable peeler to peel fruits such as kiwis, and mangoes. With the sharp knife, peel the honeydew, cantaloupe, pineapple, and prickly pears.

2. Cut the fruit into bite-sized pieces. Place the cut fruit into a large serving bowl and stir, or layer each fruit in a trifle bowl. You may also serve in individual dessert glasses.

3. Drizzle the pomegranate syrup over the fruits and sprinkle pomegranate arils on top.

Estimated prep time: 15 – 30 minutes

Parve • Yield: servings vary depending on amount of fruits used

YOM KIPPUR

Yom Kippur is the holiest day of the Jewish year and the final day of the Aseret Yemei Teshuvah, the Ten Days of Repentance that began with Rosh Hashanah. From sundown on Yom Kippur Eve and through nightfall the following day, Jews abstain from eating and drinking. They pray and turn their eyes, hearts, and souls toward Heaven, requesting that justice be offset with mercy and that the new year will be one of peace and happiness. At a climactic moment during the prayer service, the formula for ensuring a good year is given. "Teshuvah — repentance, tefillah — prayer, and tzeddakah — charity avert the evil decree." By following this timeless "recipe" for success in our lives, we can return home from the synagogue after a long day devoted to fervent prayer, inspired and full of hope for the upcoming year.

With this in mind as we prepare spiritually for this awe-inspiring day, we can use our crafting talents to create beautiful objects to help us achieve these goals. A "Midot and Mitzvah Journal" is an excellent tool to help focus on repentance, while a prayer bookmark inscribed with an inspirational verse from the Yom Kippur machzor, the book of prayers for this holy day, can add a special feeling.

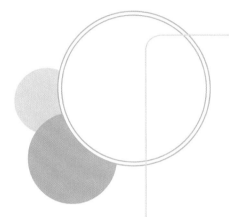

A sachet is a small bag made of fabric and filled with dried flowers, herbs, and/or spices. On Yom Kippur, when you are fasting and feel weak, their sweet smell will invigorate you.

After Yom Kippur the sachets can be placed on hangers or in drawers. They will give your clothing a wonderful scent.

sweet-scented sachets

What you will need:

- ☐ ruler
- ☐ 2½"-3"-wide ribbon or lace
- ☐ pinking shears
- ☐ needle and thread
- ☐ potpourri, dried lavender, cloves and/or cinnamon sticks
- ☐ scissors
- ☐ narrow ribbon or cord

How to do it:

1. For each sachet, measure a 12" piece of ribbon. Cut with pinking shears. Place the ribbon on a table or other work surface with the plain side of the ribbon on the table and the pretty side facing you.

2. Fold the ribbon in half so that both ends touch. It should look like a pouch. With the needle and thread, stitch together the two sides of the ribbon, using a running stitch or back stitch. (See page 264 for instructions for these stitches.) When you have sewn both edges, turn the pouch inside-out so that the pretty side is showing.

3. Fill the ribbon pouch ¾ full with a mixture of potpourri, dried lavender, cloves, and cinnamon sticks. You can use all or only one of these ingredients.

4. Measure and cut a 10" piece of ribbon or cord; tightly tie the sachet closed.

Estimated time: 15 minutes per sachet

This bookmark is ideal for keeping the place in your machzor (holiday prayerbook) on Yom Kippur. Choose a meaningful sentence from the Yom Kippur prayers to stay focused on the awesomeness of this day.

prayerbook bookmark

What you will need:

- [ ] ruler and pencil
- [ ] 1 (12"x12") sheet cardstock or thick scrapbook paper
- [ ] scissors
- [ ] 1 piece patterned scrapbook paper
- [ ] pinking shears
- [ ] fine tip markers
- [ ] glue stick
- [ ] hole puncher
- [ ] 2 reinforcements (or eyelet and eyelet setter)
- [ ] assorted narrow ribbons

How to do it:

1. With your ruler and pencil, measure a 2½"x6" rectangle of cardstock or thick paper. Use the scissors to cut out the rectangle.

2. With your ruler and pencil, measure a 2"x5½" rectangle of patterned scrapbook paper. Cut it out with the pinking shears.

3. Using a pencil, write your chosen sentence on the patterned scrapbook paper. Then trace over the letters with markers.

4. Use the glue stick to glue the patterned paper with the sentence to the cardstock, leaving a narrow, even border around the edges.

5. Punch a hole in the top center of the bookmark, ½" from the top edge. Place reinforcements or eyelet (follow eyelet setting instructions that come with your eyelet setter tool) around the hole. Thread 3–4 ribbons through the hole. Knot a small piece of ribbon around the ribbons near the top of the bookmark; this will form a tassel and hold the ribbons together. Trim the ends of the tassel.

Estimated time: 10 minutes

אבינו מלכנו,
חננו וענני
כי אין בנו
מעשים, עשה
עמני צדקה
וחסד והושיענו

I love journal writing. Writing about my day, reflecting on my actions, and setting down goals for the days ahead helps me in my interactions and behavior toward others. The Ten Days of Atonement are a special time to reflect on our past behavior, admit to our mistakes, and take upon ourselves not to repeat our past transgressions in the future — these are three components of teshuvah (repentance).

A "Midot and Mitzvot Journal" can be helpful to you. It is a private place to record which *midot* (character traits) and mitzvot you are good at and in which areas you wish to improve.

midot and mitzvot journal

What you will need:

- ☐ pencil
- ☐ 1 notebook
- ☐ 2 (8½"x11" or 12"x12") sheets of coordinating patterned scrapbook paper
- ☐ scissors or paper cutter
- ☐ tape runner or glue stick
- ☐ marker, optional
- ☐ small tag or scrap of scrapbook paper, decorative buttons, or stickers, optional

How to do it:

1. Use the pencil to trace the front cover of the notebook onto the back of a sheet of scrapbook paper. Cut out the traced shape using scissors or a paper cutter.

2. For the back cover of the notebook, repeat step 1, using the second sheet of paper. Save scraps to make the optional tag, below.

3. Use a tape runner or glue stick to attach the cut papers to the front and back of the notebook. Smooth out any air bubbles so that the paper is flat against the notebook.

Optional: Use a marker to write "My Midot and Mitzvot Journal" on a decorative tag or scrap of coordinating paper. Glue the tag to the front of the notebook. Decorate the tag by gluing on small buttons or stickers

Estimated time: 15 minutes – 30 minutes

Giving tzeddakah (charity) is important all year long. It has extra significance at this time of year. This tzeddakah box holder is a great way to organize your pushkas (tzeddakah boxes). Keep it out on the kitchen counter, or in some other central place, to remind you to empty your pockets of loose change and place it into a pushka.

tzeddakah box holder

What you will need:

- [ ] ruler and pencil
- [ ] shoe box
- [ ] patterned contact paper or fabric contact paper, we used Delta FabriCraft
- [ ] scissors
- [ ] 1 yard (¼"-½" wide) ribbon
- [ ] glue gun and glue sticks
- [ ] permanent marker, optional

How to do it:

1. Use the ruler to measure the perimeter of the shoe box. Cut 2 pieces of contact paper approximately ½" wider and ½" longer than the box. Set aside. Trace the bottom of the box onto another piece of contact paper and cut out.

2. Following the instructions on the back of the contact paper, stick one long piece around the inside of the box, smoothing out any air bubbles. There should be extra contact paper sticking up at the top of the box. Fold the contact paper over the top edge, sticking it down to the outer sides of the box. Use your scissors to snip in at the corners so that the contact paper folds down neatly.

3. Take the second long piece of contact paper and apply it to the outer sides of the box. Tuck the extra contact paper under the box and stick to the bottom of the box, snipping in at the corners if necessary.

4. Apply the contact paper rectangle to the inside of the box.

5. Use a glue gun and glue sticks to adhere the ribbon to the top of the box.

6. If you like, use a permanent marker to write your favorite tzeddakah quotation on the outside of the holder.

Estimated time: 20 – 30 minutes

⋯⋯⋯ kreplach ⋯⋯⋯

Kreplach are small meat- or chicken-filled dough packets that are usually boiled and served with soup. They are traditionally eaten on Erev Yom Kippur because the filling is hidden inside the dough, just like Hashem's judgment is hidden from us.

What you will need:

- ☐ measuring cups and spoons
- ☐ food processor
- ☐ large mixing bowl
- ☐ large pot
- ☐ sharp knife and cutting board
- ☐ frying pan
- ☐ wooden spoon or silicone spatula
- ☐ pastry board
- ☐ rolling pin
- ☐ 3" round cookie cutter or drinking glass
- ☐ fork
- ☐ slotted spoon
- ☐ baking sheet
- ☐ ziplock freezer bag

Dough Ingredients:

- ☐ 2 eggs
- ☐ 3 tablespoons water
- ☐ 2 cups flour plus more for sprinkling
- ☐ ½ teaspoon salt

Filling Ingredients:

- ☐ 2 tablespoons oil
- ☐ 1 onion
- ☐ 1 cup boiled chicken
- ☐ 1 teaspoon salt
- ☐ 1 tablespoon chopped parsley, optional

How to do it:

1. Place eggs and water into food processor. Using the S-blade, process for 1 minute. Add flour and salt. Process on high until dough forms a ball.

2. Place the dough into the large mixing bowl and set aside to rest.

3. Fill a large pot halfway with water and bring to a boil.

4. Meanwhile, using a sharp knife and cutting board, cut the onion into small pieces. Place the oil into a frying pan and heat over medium heat. Add the onion to the frying pan. Sauté for 5-8 minutes, until onions are slightly brown. Stir often with the wooden spoon or spatula.

4. Wash and dry the food processor bowl. Combine chicken (make sure that all bones are removed), onions, and salt in the food processor bowl. Process into a smooth mixture. Add chopped parsley, optional.

5. Sprinkle flour onto a clean counter or pastry board. Place dough on the floured surface and use the rolling pin to roll dough to ¼" thickness.

6. With a cookie cutter or drinking glass, cut out circles of dough. Cut the circles close together. Reroll dough scraps and cut out more circles.

7. Place 1-2 teaspoons of filling in the center of each dough circle. Fold the circles over the filling. Press the tines of a fork around the edges to seal.

8. When the water in the pot comes to a boil, reduce heat so that the water is only simmering (there should be only tiny bubbles in the water). Drop the kreplach gently into the simmering water and cook for 15 minutes or until they float to the top of the water.

9. Remove the kreplach from the water with a slotted spoon and place on a baking sheet to cool. Serve the kreplach in your favorite soup.

Note: When kreplach have cooled, they can be frozen in one layer on a baking sheet. When frozen, remove from baking sheet and store in a ziplock freezer bag.

Estimated prep time: 45 minutes – 1 hour

Cook time: 15 minutes

Meat • Yield: 18 kreplach

potato leek soup

- ☐ sharp knife
- ☐ cutting board
- ☐ measuring spoons
- ☐ large pot
- ☐ wooden spoon
- ☐ vegetable peeler
- ☐ liquid measuring cup
- ☐ immersion blender

Ingredients:

- ☐ 3 large leeks
- ☐ 2 tablespoons oil
- ☐ 6 potatoes
- ☐ 8 cups water
- ☐ 1 tablespoon salt
- ☐ ⅛ teaspoon pepper

This creamy white soup has a bit of a sophisticated look and taste. I like serving it before a fast because it's filling and light at the same time. Place 1 or 2 warm kreplach in each bowl before serving.

How to do it:

1. With a sharp knife, cut off the dark green leafy parts and the root ends of the leeks. On a cutting board, slice each leek in half lengthwise. Wash the leeks very well, opening the leaves under running water to remove the dirt between them.

2. Slice each leek half horizontally into narrow half-moons.

3. Place 2 tablespoons oil into a large pot and place over medium heat. When the oil sizzles, add the sliced leeks. Lower the heat and cook, uncovered, until they are soft. Stir often with a wooden spoon to make sure they are not burning.

4. With a vegetable peeler, peel the potatoes. Using a sharp knife and cutting board, cut the potatoes into chunks.

5. When the leeks are really soft, add the potatoes and water. Turn up the heat to medium. Cook, uncovered, for 45 minutes. Add the salt and pepper.

6. Turn off the heat and let the soup cool for 15 minutes.

7. When the soup has cooled slightly, blend the soup with an immersion blender until it is smooth and creamy.

Estimated prep time: 20 – 30 minutes
Cook time: 45 minutes
Parve • Yield: 8 servings

power smoothies

What you will need:

- ☐ blender
- ☐ liquid measuring cup
- ☐ knife
- ☐ spoon
- ☐ measuring spoons

Strawberry-Mango Smoothie Ingredients:

- ☐ 1 (8-ounce) container vanilla yogurt
- ☐ 1 cup frozen strawberries, not in syrup
- ☐ ½ cup frozen mango
- ☐ 1 cup orange juice
- ☐ ½ cup crushed ice

Banana-Cherry Smoothie Ingredients:

- ☐ 1 (8-ounce) container vanilla yogurt or cherry vanilla yogurt
- ☐ 2 bananas
- ☐ 1 cup frozen cherries
- ☐ 1 cup apple juice
- ☐ ½ cup crushed ice

Smoothies (see photo on page 61) are a refreshing treat after fasting. Aside from quenching your thirst, they provide vitamins, minerals, and a boost of energy. Keep packages of frozen fruits in the freezer so that you can whip up these smoothies in no time for everyone to enjoy. They're great for breakfast, too.

How to do it:

Strawberry-Mango Smoothies:

1. Slightly thaw frozen strawberries and mango.
2. Place the vanilla yogurt, strawberries, mango, orange juice, and ice into the blender. Cover the blender tightly with the blender cover. Blend on medium-high setting until smooth.
3. Pour smoothies into tall glasses and serve.

Banana-Cherry Smoothies:

1. Slightly thaw frozen cherries.
2. Peel and slice the bananas and place into the blender. Add the remaining ingredients. Cover the blender tightly with the blender cover. Blend on a medium-high setting until smooth.
3. Pour smoothies into tall glasses and serve.

Estimated prep time: 5 minutes
Dairy • Yield: 2 – 3 servings of each smoothie

break-the-fast muffins

What you will need:

- ☐ measuring cups and spoons
- ☐ 1 large and 1 small mixing bowl
- ☐ spoon and fork
- ☐ 12-cup muffin tray
- ☐ paper muffin cups
- ☐ spatula
- ☐ shallow bowl or plate
- ☐ small pot or microwave-safe bowl
- ☐ wire rack

Muffin Ingredients:

- ☐ 1 cup flour
- ☐ ½ cup oatmeal
- ☐ ½ cup sugar
- ☐ 1½ teaspoons baking powder
- ☐ ⅛ teaspoon salt
- ☐ 1 egg
- ☐ ½ cup milk or soy milk (orange juice can also be substituted for a slightly sweeter taste)
- ☐ ⅓ cup vegetable oil

Topping Ingredients:

- ☐ ¼ cup sugar
- ☐ 1 teaspoon cinnamon
- ☐ ¼ cup melted butter or margarine

Enjoy these delicious muffins after the fast. They taste just as good the day after you baked them as they do straight from the oven. If you want the "just from the oven taste," warm them in the microwave or toaster oven.

How to do it:

1. Preheat the oven to 350°F.

2. In the large mixing bowl, combine the flour, oatmeal, sugar, baking powder, and salt. Stir with a spoon to combine.

3. In the small mixing bowl, combine the egg, milk, and oil. Mix with a fork.

4. Add the egg mixture to the flour mixture. Stir until the flour mixture is just moistened — it's okay if it is still lumpy. Don't overmix.

5. Line the muffin tray with paper muffin cups. Fill the cups ¾ full of batter.

6. Place the tray into the hot oven and bake for 20-25 minutes.

7. While the muffins are baking, prepare the topping. Mix the sugar and cinnamon together in a shallow bowl.

8. Melt the butter in a small pot over low heat or melt in a microwave-safe bowl for approximately one minute, until completely melted. Carefully remove the pot from the heat or the bowl from the microwave. Let cool slightly.

9. Remove muffins from oven when done. Dip the tops of the hot muffins into the melted butter and then into the cinnamon-sugar mixture. Let the muffins cool on a wire rack or serve while still warm.

Estimated prep time: 10 minutes
Bake time: 20 – 25 minutes
Dairy or Parve • Yield: 1 dozen

SUCCOT

Built from plywood, fiberglass, or canvas — there's nothing quite like a succah, our temporary "home away from home" that commemorates the "booths" that God created for the Jews in the desert after they had left Egypt. Decorations glitter in the candlelight and the sound of happy singing is heard through the bamboo or leafy s'chach that serves as its roof.

Succot is tailor-made for "do-it-yourself-ers" who love building forts or home additions and who feel more at home on a ladder than on the ground. However, even if you prefer to build on a smaller scale with blocks or Legos, this holiday is just right for you, too. For many people, the really fun part is decorating the succah! You can craft decorations such as unique hanging flower balls, a mini-succah diorama, or a "Welcome" sign. Whatever you choose, you'll feel even happier during this "time of our rejoicing" surrounded by your family's own creations.

As Succot ends, we greet the wonderful holiday of Simchat Torah, during which the congregation celebrates the cycle of Torah readings. They circle the bimah (lectern) with the Torah scrolls to the fanfare of waving flags, stamping feet, and voices raised in song. Proudly joining the circle of dancers, children will be thrilled to display the flags that they created and to hold their very own cuddly Torahs made of felt!

Reciting a blessing and shaking the lulav and etrog are among the special mitzvot of Succot. Etrogim often come from Israel, wrapped well and stored in a cardboard box. While the cardboard box is a perfectly fine place for keeping your etrog, it can be even nicer to have a beautiful etrog box that you crafted yourself in which to place your etrog.

etrog box

What you will need:

- [ ] sandpaper
- [ ] 3"x6" hinged wooden craft box or index card box
- [ ] paper towel
- [ ] silver metallic acrylic paint
- [ ] paper or disposable plastic plate
- [ ] 1 (1"-1½") paintbrush
- [ ] 1 (2-ounce) package oven bake clay, any color (we used Sculpey)
- [ ] skewer or toothpick
- [ ] craft glue, or glue gun and glue sticks
- [ ] gold paint marker, optional

How to do it:

1. Use the sandpaper to sand the edges of the box to make sure they are completely smooth. Wipe off any dust with a damp paper towel.

2. Squeeze a large amount of silver metallic acrylic paint onto a plate. Use your paintbrush to paint the inside and outside of the box. If you prefer a darker color, let the first coat of paint dry and then paint on a second coat. Allow the box to dry completely.

3. Take the clay and soften it by rolling it and pulling it. (The warmth of your hands will soften it so that you can work it.) Shape the clay into an oval and then form it into the shape of an etrog. Use a skewer or toothpick to press lines and bumps into the clay. Bake the clay according to the directions on the package.

4. After the clay etrog cools, paint it with the silver paint and let dry. When it is dry, use craft glue or a glue gun and glue sticks to attach the etrog to the center of the box cover.

Optional: Using a gold paint marker, decorate the lid with your favorite Succot phrase.

Estimated time: 30 minutes
Baking time: approximately 15 – 20 minutes
Cooling time: 15 minutes
Drying time: 1 – 2 hours

Hanging this cheerful welcome sign on the door of your succah will let friends and relatives know how happy you are to have them join you.

felt welcome sign

What you will need:

- [ ] ruler and pencil or chalk
- [ ] scissors
- [ ] stiffened felt pieces in assorted colors, including brown or beige and green
- [ ] 12"x18" piece of stiffened felt
- [ ] white craft glue
- [ ] embroidery needle and green embroidery thread
- [ ] 10-12 small round and/or flower shaped buttons
- [ ] hole puncher
- [ ] two medium buttons
- [ ] 2-foot piece of ribbon, cut with pinking shears
- [ ] metallic dimensional fabric paint

How to do it:

1. To make the succah, use the ruler and pencil or chalk to measure a 5"x9" rectangle from the felt. Use the scissors to cut it out, and cut a square opening in the middle of the rectangle (see photo).

2. Trace the square onto the back of a different-colored piece of felt and cut out the traced square.

3. Center the rectangle on the 12"x18" piece of stiffened felt and use the craft glue to glue it down. Glue the square into the rectangle's opening.

4. Cut a few strips of beige or brown felt to resemble s'chach. Glue the strips to the top of the succah. Cut a few leaf shapes out of green felt and glue on to the s'chach.

5. Thread the embroidery needle with the green thread. With a pencil or chalk, draw a straight line level with the succah's lower edge as a guide for embroidering the grass. Embroider straight lines of varying lengths on either side of the succah to resemble grass (see photo). When finished, erase pencil or chalk line.

6. Glue a few round or flower-shaped buttons to the top of several "blades" of "grass."

7. Punch a hole, 2" in from the side and 1" down from the top, on each side of the top of the sign. Thread the ribbon through the holes. Knot the ribbon ends to secure the ribbon in the hole. Glue a medium button over each knot, covering it completely.

8. Use a pencil to outline the letters for "Welcome" or "ברוכים הבאים" on the center of the lower edge of the sign (see photo).

9. Trace the outlined letters with metallic dimensional fabric paint and let dry.

Estimated time: 45 minutes – 1 hour
Drying time: as recommended on the fabric paint bottle

While shopping in my local craft store before Succot, I started trading succah decorating tips with some fellow shoppers. One woman had a shopping cart loaded to the rim with fake flowers that she said she would be using to make hanging flower balls. I loved the idea and quickly loaded my cart with flowers as well — luckily, the fall flowers are usually discounted around this time of year. These flower balls are magnificent — I thank my "anonymous friend" for this lovely project.

hanging flower balls

What you will need:

- ☐ 2 bunches large faux sunflowers or other flowers of your choice
- ☐ 5" Styrofoam ball
- ☐ glue gun and glue sticks
- ☐ 24" piece of 1"-1½"-wide grosgrain ribbon
- ☐ scissors
- ☐ T-pin or large paperclip

How to do it:

1. Separate the flower heads from the stems (they should come off easily).

2. Squeeze a dab of hot glue from the glue gun onto the back of a flower and quickly glue the flower to the Styrofoam ball before the hot glue dries. Continue gluing flowers to the ball in this manner. Be sure to glue the flowers close together; it's okay if the petals overlap slightly.

3. When the ball is completely covered with flowers, check to be sure that there are no empty spaces that allow the Styrofoam to show. If there are, cut several leaves from the stems and glue them to the ball to cover the empty spots.

4. To hang the flower ball: Loop the ribbon over a succah beam or piece of bamboo so that the two ends of ribbon hang down evenly. Place a T-pin or a bent paper clip through both ends of the ribbon and pin the ribbon into the ball. (It's easier to do this if one person holds the ball while another person pins it in.)

Tip: Your succah will look beautiful if you make a variety of hanging balls using different-sized balls and colorful flowers. Hang them from ribbons of varying lengths throughout the succah.

Estimated time: 20 minutes

As a child I loved "building" my own succah using a shoe box and arranging doll furniture and paper chains and decorations inside. Create your own succah diorama using bits and pieces of doll furniture, scraps of colored paper, and leftovers from other craft projects. We made the miniature "food" out of polymer clay. Use your imagination; this is your chance to build the succah of your dreams!

mini succah

What you will need:

- [ ] large shoe box, without cover
- [ ] wood-grain contact paper
- [ ] 1 sheet self-adhesive stiffened felt
- [ ] small twigs, artificial or fallen leaves, rosemary sprigs, and/or bamboo place mat
- [ ] glue or scotch tape
- [ ] scissors
- [ ] miniature table and chairs
- [ ] decorating materials, such as: scraps of colored paper, felt, velvet, lace, pompoms, ribbons, sequins, buttons, stickers, small photos, magazine pictures, fake flowers, polymer clay
- [ ] 1 sheet clear acetate or gallon-sized ziplock bag

How to do it:

1. Stand the shoe box on its side on your work surface so that the opening of the box faces you (see photo).

2. Measure and cut two identical pieces of contact paper to fit around the two short sides and the back of the box. Following the instructions on the contact paper, attach one of the pieces to the outside and the other piece to the inside of the box.

3. Measure one long side of the box and trace it onto the back of the felt. Cut out the felt rectangle and glue it to the inside bottom of the box. This will be the succah floor.

4. Spread glue across the top of the box and glue on place mat, twigs, leaves, and/or rosemary sprigs so that they resemble s'chach. Let dry.

5. While glue dries, craft decorations out of your decorating materials.

6. Glue or tape the decorations to the interior "walls" and "ceiling" of the mini succah.

7. Glue or tape doll furniture to the "floor" of the succah.

8. Tape the sheet of clear acetate over the opening of the succah, or cut off the top of the ziplock bag and cut the bag into two pieces. Cut one piece of plastic to the size of your box and tape it over the box opening.

Estimated time: 1 hour

Your entire family can join together to make this striking succah wall hanging. Rolling the tissue paper squares into balls is a great group activity, and even very young children can join in the fun.

lulav and etrog wall hanging

What you will need:

- ☐ 1 (12"x12") sheet of thin cardboard or cardstock (we used the cardboard backing from a pad of scrapbook paper)
- ☐ pencil
- ☐ 1 sheet each: dark green, light green, beige, and yellow tissue paper
- ☐ 5 small bowls or plates
- ☐ scissors
- ☐ craft glue
- ☐ small bowl and narrow paintbrush
- ☐ dark green yarn or 2 dark green pipe cleaners
- ☐ light green yarn or 3 light green pipe cleaners
- ☐ marker
- ☐ 1 whole clove

How to do it:

1. Photocopy the lulav and etrog templates (pages 258, 259, 261). Cut out the lulav and etrog. Use a pencil to trace them onto the cardboard positioned in a diamond shape in front of you, with the lulav in the center (see photo). Draw three lines extending from the right of the lulav holder and two lines extending from the left.

2. Cut each sheet of tissue paper into 1-inch squares. Crumple and roll each square into a ball shape. As you work, place the tissue paper balls into bowls, using 1 bowl per color.

3. Pour craft glue into a small bowl. With the paintbrush, coat the entire lulav holder on the cardboard with a thick layer of glue. Glue on the beige tissue paper balls, covering the holder completely. Brush three evenly spaced horizontal lines of glue onto the lulav drawing to form the rings that bind the lulav together (see photo). Glue beige tissue paper balls to cover rings completely.

4. Coat the lulav area with a thick coat of glue and glue the light green tissue paper balls to it.

5. Brush small dabs of glue around the three penciled lines to resemble hadasim. Glue the light green balls onto the glued areas. Brush a line of glue down the center of each hadas and place a piece of light green yarn or a pipe cleaner over the glue line.

6. Repeat step 6, using the dark green balls and the dark green yarn or pipe cleaners for the two aravoth on the left side.

7. Brush a thick coat of glue over the entire outlined etrog. Glue all the yellow tissue paper balls to cover the etrog. Make sure not to leave any empty spots. Glue the clove to the top of the etrog.

8. Use a pencil to outline the letters for Lulav v'Etrog in Hebrew or English. Go over the letters with a marker. Erase any pencil lines.

Estimated time: 45 minutes – 1 hour

This stunning chain is simple to make and can be customized to your decorating taste by using the ribbons and fake fruits of your choosing.

ribbon bow and fruit chain

What you will need:

- ☐ long cording or thin ribbon
- ☐ fake fruit with stems and/or berry picks
- ☐ ¼"–½"-wide ribbons of your choice; sheer ribbons work best
- ☐ scissors

How to do it:

1. Decide how long you would like your chain to be and cut a piece of cording or ribbon 12 inches longer than that length.

2. Knot a small length of ribbon tightly to the stem of a fruit and tie the other end around the cording. Continue to tie additional fruits on to the cording in this manner, at approximately 3-inch intervals. If you are using berry picks, bend the end of the pick around the cording until it is securely attached to the cording.

3. Tie ribbons into bows between fruits.

4. To hang the chain, loop each end around a succah beam or piece of bamboo and knot securely into place.

Estimated time: 30 minutes

Tips for Hanging Decorations and Keeping Decorations Dry:

Since a succah is a temporary outdoor structure, it can be a tough task to hang all the lovely decorations and keep them dry, especially in the Northeast, where I live. Here are tips to help make it easy and effective.

Hanging Decorations: When you hang posters or pictures, be sure to use removable adhesives, such as FunTac, Scotch Removable Mounting Squares, or Removable Poster Tape. Place small balls of FunTac on the back corners of hanging pictures and press against the wall so that they stay in place. Adhesive Velcro dots and strips work well on canvas succot.

Heavy artwork should be hung from the succah frame. Screw 2 eye hooks into the back of the framed artwork, thread clear fishing line through the hooks, loop the ends over the succah frame, and knot ends.

Keeping Decorations Dry: Laminate posters at office or teacher-supply stores. Another option is to cover the front and back of artwork with clear contact paper. This is great for bulky items or crayoned pictures, because crayon can melt in a laminating machine. Place fragile or framed artwork in a protected area if possible (such as against the wall of your house, where there may be a roof overhang).

You can also place artwork into a ziplock bag, press out all the air, and seal. Tape the excess to the back of your picture.

When my daughter was in Morah Ellen's class in Bais Yaakov of Queens, she made this beautiful flag for Simchat Torah. I had never seen such an unusual flag before and immediately knew that I wanted to craft this project as well. The overhead projector transparencies can be found in most craft, office, and school-supply stores.

"stained glass" flag

What you will need:

- ☐ scissors
- ☐ 1 piece shiny paper
- ☐ pencil
- ☐ metallic marker
- ☐ decoupage medium, such as Mod Podge
- ☐ 2 (8½"x11") overhead projector transparencies
- ☐ pastel-colored tissue paper
- ☐ paper clips
- ☐ hole puncher
- ☐ wooden dowel or round cardboard stick from dry cleaners clothes hanger (you can paint it first to match your flag)
- ☐ glue gun and glue sticks
- ☐ pastel yarn

How to do it:

1. Photocopy and cut out the Torah template (page 262). Trace the Torah twice onto the back of the shiny paper and cut out the two traced Torahs. Use the metallic marker to write "Simchat Torah" or your favorite Simchat Torah phrase on the front of each Torah.

2. Coat the front of one Torah with a thin coat of Mod Podge and glue it to the center of a transparency.

3. Take 3 or 4 large pieces of tissue paper and cut into 2" squares (approximately — they don't have to be perfectly straight).

4. Working with a small area at a time, spread a thin coat of Mod Podge on the transparency and place tissue paper squares on the coated area, overlapping slightly. Continue spreading Mod Podge and sticking on squares, until the transparency is covered. Let dry.

5. Coat the back of second Torah with a thin coat of Mod Podge; glue it to the back of the Torah on the first transparency. Let dry.

6. Place the second transparency to the back of the paper-covered transparency and clip together with several paper clips.

7. With the hole puncher, punch holes, ½"–1" apart, around the outer edge of the whole flag.

8. Line up the dowel with the top left corner of the flag. Carefully separate the transparencies slightly and insert the dowel between them; glue into place with the glue gun and glue sticks.

9. Double a long piece of yarn and knot one end. Thread into the hole at the top left corner of the flag. Weave yarn through holes around the dowel and continue around the rest of the flag, removing paper clip as you weave. Knot the yarn and trim.

Estimated time: 1 hour, divided
Drying time: 4 – 6 hour, divided

This delightful flag is the perfect size for small hands to hold while dancing in shul on Simchat Torah. The glittery design will capture everyone's attention, and the pompom on top is there to ensure that no one's eye is accidentally poked by the stick.

mini flag

What you will need:

- ☐ 1 (12"x18") sheet stiffened felt in the color of your choice
- ☐ pencil
- ☐ scissors
- ☐ craft glue or glittering glue with brush
- ☐ glitter in assorted colors
- ☐ paper plates
- ☐ double-sided red liner tape (we used Provo Craft Terrifically Tacky Tape)
- ☐ X-Acto knife
- ☐ chopstick or small dowel
- ☐ large pompom
- ☐ metallic dimensional fabric paint
- ☐ curling ribbon, optional

How to do it:

1. Cut the stiffened felt into a 7"x9" rectangle. Brush a thin line of glue around 3 edges of the flag. Working over a paper plate, cover the glued areas with glitter and shake the excess onto the paper plate. Pour the extra glitter back into the container.

2. Cut a 1"x2" rectangle of the double-sided adhesive sheet and stick the shape onto the left side of the flag to form the Torah.

3. Peel the top paper from the adhesive rectangle and sprinkle glitter on. Shake off any excess over a paper plate.

4. Use strips of tape to craft the top strip of the Torah cover and the top and bottom handles (see photo). Add glitter as in step 3.

5. Use the X-Acto knife to cut a ½" horizontal slit near the top and bottom of the left side of the flag. Thread the dowel through the slits. Spread some craft glue on top of the dowel and glue a large pompom to the top. Let dry.

6. Use a pencil to outline the letters "שמחת תורה" in the center of the flag.

7. Trace and fill in the outlined letters with fabric paint and let dry.

Optional: Tie strands of curling ribbon around the top of the dowel, under the pompom. To curl the ribbon, pull each ribbon strand against the blade of the scissors.

Estimated time: 30 minutes

Drying time: as recommended on the fabric paint bottle

This cuddly, soft Torah is easy for young children to craft, either by sewing or gluing the pieces together. Their pride in their work will be evident when they dance with it on Simchat Torah.

felt Torah

What you will need:

- ☐ 2 (12"x18") sheets of felt, in the color of your choice
- ☐ pen or marker
- ☐ scissors
- ☐ metallic dimensional fabric paint
- ☐ straight pins
- ☐ large embroidery needle and embroidery thread, or glue gun and glue sticks, or fabric glue
- ☐ polyester fiberfill
- ☐ trim, optional

How to do it:

1. Photocopy Torah template (page 259) and cut out.

2. Trace the Torah shape onto the backs of both pieces of felt. Cut out the felt Torahs.

3. Use fabric paint to decorate the front of one of the felt pieces. Let dry for the time recommended on the fabric paint bottle.

4. Use straight pins to pin the two pieces of felt together, one on top of the other, painted side up. Thread the embroidery needle and use a blanket stitch to sew the Torahs together on three sides. (See page 264 for instructions on how to work a blanket stitch.)

5. Stuff the Torah with the polyester fiberfill. Sew up the last side. Or, use a glue gun and glue sticks or fabric glue to glue the felt pieces together leaving one side open; stuff with polyester fiberfill and glue the last side shut.

Optional: Use fabric glue to attach trim to the top and bottom of the Torah (see back Torah in photo).

Estimated time: 1 hour
Drying time: up to 24 hours

SUCCAH HOP

For many families, a favorite Succot activity is their annual "Succah Hop." Adults and kids "hop" from one neighbor's or friend's succah to another, eat a sweet or two in each succah, and have a chance to see others' beautifully decorated succot. You can arrange a neighborhood Succah Hop of your own with your family and friends. End off the visit with some Succot-themed refreshments in your succah.

■ Set up:

Since most succahs aren't that large, it is important to maximize your space. Set the succah table along one wall. This will serve as your buffet table. If possible, set a smaller table next to the large one and use it for drinks and cups, since everyone will be thirsty after all that walking. Place enough chairs for all your guests around the perimeter of the succah.

For an easy centerpiece that reflects the fact that Succot is a harvest festival, pile gourds, melons, apples, and squash into baskets, colanders, buckets, or pails. Place them down the center of your table, tucking in pretty autumn leaves from your yard as well. Wrap a spoon, knife, and fork in a pretty napkin and tie with a bit of twine or string. Tuck in a berry pick or faux flower. Place the wrapped silverware bundles into empty buckets on either side of the centerpiece.

■ Food:

A make-your-own pasta salad bar is a real crowd-pleaser because everyone can customize the dish to his or her taste. Since it can be quite chilly eating in the succah on a crisp fall day, start off with a hearty vegetable soup served in mugs. A warm butternut squash kugel (see facing page) served alongside the pasta and fixings will be enjoyed by all those fulfilling the mitzvah of eating in a succah. Finish off the meal with our apple-pear gallete (page 86) for dessert.

Set up the make-your-own pasta bar as follows:

Cook two or three different types of pasta according to the package directions. Drain the pasta and place into large bowls. Add two tablespoons of olive oil to the hot pasta and season with salt and pepper. Mix well.

Place grape tomatoes, baby corn, peas, strips of pepper, mushrooms, cubed salami, cubed smoked turkey, pine nuts, and slivered almonds into bowls. Place all the bowls on the table, along with purchased Italian salad dressing and parve pesto.

butternut squash kugel

What you will need:

- [ ] large glass mixing bowl
- [ ] whisk
- [ ] measuring cups and spoons
- [ ] liquid measuring cup
- [ ] 2 quart oven-to-table baking dish or 12 (4-ounce) ramekins
- [ ] spatula

Ingredients:

- [ ] 3 eggs
- [ ] 1½ cups vanilla-flavored soy milk or rice milk
- [ ] ⅓ cup sugar
- [ ] ½ cup flour
- [ ] ½ teaspoon cinnamon
- [ ] 24 ounces frozen butternut or winter squash, defrosted and mashed
- [ ] baking spray

After trying it once, you'll see that this orange kugel will make a regular appearance on your Shabbat and Yom Tov table. Even those kids who say they "hate" vegetables love this kugel.

How to do it:

1. Preheat oven to 350°F.
2. Crack the eggs and place into the mixing bowl. Beat the eggs with the whisk until they are pale yellow and fluffy.
3. Whisk in the soy milk and sugar. Slowly add the flour. Continue whisking the batter well as you add the flour, so that there should be no lumps. Mix in the cinnamon.
4. Slowly add the mashed, defrosted squash. Mix the squash into the batter until the entire mixture is very smooth.
5. Spray the inside of the baking dish or ramekins with baking spray. Use your spatula to scrape the batter from the bowl into the dish or ramekins. Smooth down the top of the batter with your spatula.
6. Bake in the oven for 1 hour. (If using ramekins, bake for 35–45 minutes.)

Estimated prep time: 10 minutes
Bake time: 1 hour for large dish; 35 – 45 minutes for ramekins
Parve • Yield: 12 servings

apple-pear gallete

- ☐ large mixing bowl
- ☐ measuring cups and spoons
- ☐ pastry cutter, optional
- ☐ rolling pin
- ☐ vegetable peeler
- ☐ sharp knife
- ☐ small bowl
- ☐ microwave-safe bowl
- ☐ cookie sheet
- ☐ pastry brush

Pastry dough Ingredients:

- ☐ 2 cups flour
- ☐ 1 tablespoon sugar
- ☐ 1 ½ sticks margarine
- ☐ ½ cup cold water

Filling Ingredients:

- ☐ 3 baking apples
- ☐ 2 ripe pears
- ☐ 3 tablespoons sugar, divided
- ☐ 1 teaspoon cinnamon
- ☐ 4 tablespoons margarine, divided

When her Hebrew teacher had her class translate recipes from English into Hebrew, my former student, Jackie, chose this recipe. She gave me a copy of the recipe because she thought I would enjoy it. It quickly became a family favorite. I modified it a bit by adding pears to the filling. It's a wonderful Succot dessert because it highlights the seasonal fall fruits.

How to do it:

1. Preheat oven to 400°F.

2. Mix flour and sugar together in the mixing bowl. Cut the 1½ sticks of margarine into slivers; add to the flour and sugar. Blend together with your fingers or the pastry cutter until the mixture looks like lumpy peas.

3. Slowly add the water and knead by hand until soft dough forms. With the rolling pin, roll the dough out into a large circle the size of a dinner plate and place dough onto the cookie sheet.

4. Use the vegetable peeler to peel apples and pears. With the sharp knife, cut out the cores. Quarter and slice the fruit. Pile the fruit slices onto the center of the dough. Leave an approximately 2" border of dough around the fruit.

5. Mix 2 tablespoons of sugar and the cinnamon in a small bowl. Sprinkle the apples and pears with this mixture. Cut 2 tablespoons margarine into small pieces and scatter the small pieces of margarine on top of the fruit.

6. Fold the dough up and around the mound of apples and pears.

7. Place remaining 2 tablespoons margarine into a microwave-safe bowl. Melt the margarine in the microwave for 30 seconds. With a pastry brush, brush the crust with the melted margarine and sprinkle remaining tablespoon sugar over the crust.

8. Bake for 45 minutes–1 hour. Remove from the oven and transfer to a serving plate. Cut into wedge-shaped servings.

Estimated prep time: 30 minutes
Bake time: 45 minutes – 1 hour
Parve • Yield: 8 servings

CHANUKAH

The lights of the menorah dance in the window. The dreidel spins. Yummy scents and familiar sounds emanate from the kitchen — latkes sizzling in oil and children laughing. Happy Chanukah!

In the midst of the dark and dreary winter comes this wonderful holiday, commemorating a bright light in Jewish history. Chanukah reminds us of the miracle of the Jewish Maccabees' victory over the armies of the Hellenists and how the Beit HaMikdash — the Holy Temple — was rededicated for use, wherein the miracle of the tiny vial of oil that burned for eight full days and nights occurred. Most of all, Chanukah celebrates the miracle of Jewish tenacity and Jewish survival.

With eight long winter nights to enjoy Chanukah, there's plenty of time for family projects. Try an interesting twist on the classic children's song, "Dreidel, dreidel, dreidel/I made it out of clay…" with a lovely clay dreidel that spins, not on the floor, but on a girl's charm bracelet! Chanukah presents are that much nicer when they come wrapped in stamped gift wrap, accompanied by a beautiful handmade card. Finally, be sure that you spend one night, at least, "doughnut-dipping," at your very special Chanukah get-together for family and friends.

Here's an interesting oil menorah for you to craft, made from items you'll find right in your kitchen. This project is a cool science experiment — watch how the oil floats on top of the water, because oil is lighter than water and therefore the two don't mix.

Note: For safety reasons, be sure that an adult is present in the room while the flames are burning.

glowing glass menorah

What you will need:

- [ ] long, narrow tray
- [ ] 8 low glass candleholders, clean glass baby food jars or shot glasses
- [ ] 1 slightly taller glass candleholder or glass jar
- [ ] glue dots
- [ ] liquid measuring cup or pitcher
- [ ] liquid food coloring
- [ ] olive oil
- [ ] floating wicks
- [ ] glass marbles, optional

How to do it:

1. Set up the tray in the place where you will be lighting your menorah, because it will be difficult to move once all the candleholders are filled with liquid.

2. Attach a glue dot to the bottom of each glass. Line up the candleholders on the tray, with the larger candleholder at one end, pressing down to adhere glasses to tray.

3. Fill a measuring cup or pitcher with water. Pour the water carefully into each cup, filling it halfway. Add 1–2 drops food coloring to each cup.

4. Pour approximately ½" olive oil into each cup. Let the oil settle on top of the water; then place a floating wick in each cup.

Optional: Before filling the candleholders, cover the tray surface with glass marbles.

Estimated time: 30 minutes

wooden block menorah

What you will need:

- 10 (1½") or 9 (1½") and 1 (1¾") wooden blocks
- rectangular piece of wood (approx. 16"x2"x¼") long enough to hold 9 of the blocks in a straight row
- 2 (1") wooden knobs
- extra-strong craft glue
- acrylic paint in assorted colors
- ½"-1"-wide paintbrushes
- nine pennies
- nine metal nuts or washers
- craft glue or decoupage medium, such as Mod Podge

How to do it:

1. Use your paintbrushes and acrylic paint to paint all the wooden pieces the colors of your choice. (One side of each wooden block does not need to be painted, as it will be glued to the base.) Let dry completely.

2. Glue the two wooden knobs to the bottom of the rectangular piece of wood, 2 inches in from either end. Let dry.

3. Glue on the blocks:
   Option 1: For a centered shamash, evenly space 9 (1½") blocks on the base and glue them on. Glue the 10th block on top of the middle block; or use the 1¾" block as the center block.
   Option 2: For a menorah with the shamash at one end, glue 9 (1½") blocks, evenly spaced, to the base. To make the shamash, either glue 2 blocks (1½") one on top of the other or use the 1¾" block, placed at either end of the base (see photo).

4. Glue a penny to the center of each block. Glue a nut to fit on top of the penny.

Estimated time: 45 minutes

Drying time: 1 – 2 hours

Picture menorah: After completing step 2, use a 1½" square craft punch to punch out squares from photos and patterned scrapbook paper. (If you don't have a square craft punch you can cut the squares using scissors or a paper cutter. Measure correctly and outline the block on the back of the paper in pencil before cutting.)

Glue the photo or paper squares to the front of the blocks with a thin layer of decoupage medium, such as Mod Podge or craft glue that has been thinned with a little bit of water. Smooth out any air bubbles with your fingers. Let dry for 20–30 minutes. Coat the paper squares with another layer of Mod Podge or thinned glue. Let dry and continue to step 3 to assemble the menorah.

Personalized menorah: After completing step 2 and the menorah has dried, glue chipboard or wooden letters onto the front of each block (or stick on alphabet stickers.) Decorate the blocks and menorah base with glitter and/or embellishments. Continue to step 3 to assemble the menorah.

With just a handful of wooden blocks, a rectangular piece of wood and two wooden knobs, you can craft an original Chanukah menorah. Personalize your creation with paint, lettering, patterned paper, and pictures. Since the menorahs are crafted of flammable materials, for safety reasons be sure that an adult is present in the room while the candles are burning, or use only as decorations.

clay dreidel charm jewelry or keychain

What you will need:

- oven bake clay (we used Sculpey) in the colors of your choice
- skewer or large sewing needle
- disposable baking sheet
- beading elastic
- keychain ring, optional
- jump rings, optional
- needlenose pliers, optional

How to do it:

1. Roll a walnut-sized piece of clay in your hands until it softens.
2. Roll the clay into a ball. Press lightly into the ball to flatten it. Turn over and press the other two sides gently to form a box shape.
3. To form the dreidel's point, pull downward on two edges of the box-shaped clay until they meet. Turn the box and pull down the other two edges until they meet and form a point.
4. To form the dreidel's handle, pull upward on the box-shaped clay. Use your fingers to round the top point into a handle.
5. Roll a piece of different-colored clay into a thin rope. Wrap part of the rope around the base of the dreidel's handle. With the rest, form the letters ש, ה, ג, נ. Place one letter gently on each side.
6. Using the skewer or needle, poke a hole through the handle's top.
7. For beads, roll pieces of clay into pea-sized balls, swirling two or more colors together. Or, roll clay into ½"-wide logs; slice into flat beads. Poke holes through beads with the skewer or needle.
8. Preheat oven to 250°F. Place the dreidel and beads onto the baking sheet and bake, following manufacturer's instructions. Remove from oven and let cool.

For the jewelry: Thread the beads and charm through a piece of elastic 3" longer than wrist measurement. Tie the elastic in a double knot. Trim the edges.

For the keychain: Thread a 6"-8" piece of elastic through the charm and tie a double knot in one end. String beads and charm onto the elastic. Double-knot the remaining end around the keychain ring and trim the ends, threading any extra elastic back into the nearest bead.

Optional: Before baking charm, open a jump ring with pliers and thread the jump ring through the hole in the charm's handle. After charm cools, thread it onto the elastic through the jump ring.

Estimated time: 30 minutes
Bake time: 15 minutes, or according to manufacturer's instructions
Cooling time: 20 minutes

"I have a little dreidel; I made it out of clay,

And when it's dry and ready, Oh! dreidel I shall play"

You can craft a clay dreidel just like the one in the song. Although it may not spin very well, it will certainly look great dangling from a necklace or keychain.

These adorable dreidels make perfect place cards for your Chanukah party and serve as sweet mementos for your guests to take home when the fun is over.

dreidel place-card party favors

What you will need for each dreidel:

- [ ] scissors
- [ ] pencil
- [ ] 12"x12" cardstock
- [ ] acetate or see-through vinyl; we cut one heavy-duty plastic sheet protector to make four dreidels
- [ ] decorative-edge scissors or pinking shears
- [ ] hole puncher
- [ ] 1 yard (3/8" wide) ribbon
- [ ] foil-wrapped chocolate Chanukah gelt
- [ ] markers or colored pens
- [ ] small decorative tag

How to do it:

1. Photocopy the dreidel template (page 255) and cut out. With a pencil, trace the dreidel template onto the cardstock.

2. Place the acetate over the cardstock and cut along the dreidel outline so that you end up with two dreidels, one of cardstock and one of acetate.

3. Trim the edges of the acetate dreidel with the decorative-edge scissors or pinking shears.

4. Place the acetate dreidel on the cardstock dreidel. Use your hole puncher to punch an evenly spaced number of holes around the edges of the dreidels.

5. Starting at the top of the dreidel, begin lacing the ribbon through most of the dreidel. Place a few chocolate coins between the acetate and cardstock and complete lacing the dreidel. Pull the ribbon end gently in order to have even lengths of ribbon to tie into a bow at the top.

6. Use a marker to write the name or initial of each guest on a tag. Thread the tag through the ribbon. Tie the ribbon so that the tag hangs from the center of the dreidel's bow.

Estimated time: 15 minutes

Wrap your Chanukah presents in your custom-made gift wrap, add a matching card, and send a gift to someone you love.

dreidel-stamped gift wrap and card

What you will need:

- [ ] permanent marker
- [ ] 3 flat expandable sponges
- [ ] dreidel-shaped cookie cutters, optional
- [ ] scissors
- [ ] bowl of water
- [ ] 1 roll craft paper or mailing paper
- [ ] acrylic or tempera paint in the colors of your choice
- [ ] disposable plastic plates
- [ ] blank cards and envelopes

How to do it:

1. Use the permanent marker to draw dreidel shapes on the sponges. (Or trace a dreidel shape from a cookie cutter onto the sponges.) Use scissors to cut out the sponge shapes.

2. Roll out the amount of paper that you would like to stamp and cut to size.

3. Squeeze or pour paint onto the plastic plates — one color per plate.

4. Soak the sponges in water so that they expand. Then, wring out the sponges. Dip one flat side of a sponge into the paint, making sure to cover the entire surface with paint.

5. Place the sponge, paint side down, on the paper. Apply pressure to sponge but don't rock it, then lift the sponge up gently.

6. Repeat steps 3 and 4 with all the colors you are using, randomly stamping the surface of the paper. Allow the paper to dry.

7. Stamp dreidels on the front of the cards the same way you did on the wrapping paper. You can stamp the envelopes, as well. Allow to dry.

Estimated time: 30 minutes – 45 minutes
Drying time: 1 hour

This tray is the perfect base for your family's menorahs, candles, wicks, and olive oil — everything you need will be organized in one place and any spills can be wiped away easily with a damp paper towel. You can decorate the tray by cutting out letters to spell "Chanukah," a Chanukah quote, or the words to "Maoz Tzur" and the blessings we say when lighting the menorah; or personalize it by gluing on family pictures.

This tray can also be utilized to serve yummy Chanukah treats, such as latkes or doughnuts.

chanukah tray

What you will need:

- large picture frame, with glass, 11"x13" or larger
- ruler
- pencil
- scrapbook paper, wrapping paper, or fabric
- scissors and/or paper cutter
- glue stick
- die-cut or other lettering, pictures, or embellishments; we used Provo Craft Cricut machine (most scrapbooking stores let you use their die cut machines for a nominal fee)
- craft glue
- 12"x18" (or larger) piece of self-adhesive felt or regular felt

How to do it:

1. Take apart the picture frame and separate the backing, glass, and frame. Put the glass and frame aside in a safe place for later. If the backing of the frame has an easel back, remove the easel leg.

2. Measure a piece of scrapbook paper, wrapping paper, or fabric to fit the backing of the frame. Trace the frame back onto the reverse side of the paper or fabric. Cut to fit. (If you are using scrapbook paper, you may need more than one sheet to fit the back of the frame.)

3. Use a glue stick to glue the paper onto the front of the backing (the side that will show through the glass).

4. Decorate the paper by gluing on lettering, pictures, and decorative embellishments of your choice.

5. Put the picture frame back together.

6. To ensure that the frame doesn't scratch the furniture, cut a piece of felt to fit the back of the frame. Turn the frame over and use craft glue to glue the felt to the back of the frame. If you are using self-adhesive felt, peel the paper from the felt and stick felt to the back of the frame.

Estimated time: 45 minutes – 1 hour

These stunning utensils are just the thing for serving your latkes with style!

I spent an exciting Chanukah day with the 5th through 8th graders in Shaarei Zion Girls' School in Piscataway, NJ crafting the servers, and all the girls loved this unusual craft.

Credit for this wonderful project goes to the Walder Education Pavilion in Chicago.

latke servers

What you will need:

- [ ] E6000 adhesive
- [ ] flat, colored glass marbles
- [ ] inexpensive all-metal serving pieces, such as a slotted spoon, pancake turner, large serving spoon
- [ ] metal wire, 22-gauge
- [ ] wire cutters or strong scissors

How to do it:

1. Use E6000 to glue 4-5 marbles to the handle of each serving piece, leaving a narrow space between each stone (see photo). Let dry.

2. Wrap the wire tightly approximately 6 times around the base of the handle, below the stone. Continue wrapping the wire in a pretty design around each stone, tightly looping the wire between them. Tightly loop the wire around the top stone. Use the wire cutter to cut the wire. Tuck the cut end in under the wire loops.

3. Let glue set for 24 hours before using utensils.

Estimated time: 15 minutes – 30 minutes
Drying time: Initial drying time: 30 minutes
Total drying time: 24 hours

DOUGHNUT & ICE-CREAM PARTY

During Chanukah, people often get together with family and friends. The great thing about Chanukah is that it is eight days long, so there's always time for another party. Even if your friends have their own family get-togethers to attend, they surely will want to come to this fun dessert party. So gather some friends and relatives and have fun at a Chanukah party that can't be "topped"!

This party is really easy and fun for the host because everyone makes his or her own dessert combinations. All you have to do is supply the ingredients and toppings, then join everyone in the fun of creating new culinary combinations. Yum!

■ Set up:

Since this party involves food preparation, set it up in the kitchen. Cover your kitchen table and/or kitchen island with a paper or plastic tablecloth (so that you can roll up and throw out the mess when you are done.) For a decorative accent, top the tablecloth with a roll of inexpensive patterned contact paper unrolled down the center of the table. This serves as an attractive, yet practical, table runner. Scatter dreidels and chocolate coins around the serving pieces. Supply your guests with disposable or cloth aprons so that their clothing won't become soiled (cloth aprons will also make great souvenirs to take home), along with bakery boxes and paper bags for transporting their decorated doughnuts and treats home — if there are any left at the end of the party.

■ Food:

Place ice-cream cones, ice cream, fudge sauce, caramel sauce, strawberry topping, sprinkles, silver dragées, crushed nuts, and whipped cream in bowls and/or cups on the table. Have ice-cream scoops, spoons, and lots of napkins handy.

For chocolate-dipped ice-cream cones:

Melt semisweet chocolate in a large microwave-safe bowl in the microwave. Dip the open end of each sugar cone partly into the chocolate and then immediately into sprinkles or nuts. Place the dipped cones upside-down on waxed paper to harden.

Prepare large platters of homemade (see page 108) or store-bought unfrosted sufganiot — an assortment of jelly, custard, and caramel doughnuts — on the island or table. Stand a little sign on or near each platter, stating what type of filling is inside. Place purchased or homemade chocolate and vanilla icing in bowls. (You can tint bowls of vanilla icing different colors by adding a drop or two of food coloring and mixing well until you get the desired color.) Put out sugar shakers filled with sprinkles, confectioner's sugar, and colored sugar. Each person can dip his or her doughnuts in the icing of choice and then add sprinkles or sugar.

Each guest can customize an ice-cream sundae or doughnut to his or her individual taste.

Play dreidel, sing Chanukah songs, and have a ball!

Estimated set-up time: 30 minutes – 1 hour

potato latkes with applesauce

These latkes (see photo, page 103) are so yummy they are usually devoured as soon as they are ready and may never make it to the table! Serve with flavored applesauce — prepare it in advance so that the latkes will be hot when served. Adult supervision needed!

What you will need:

- [ ] vegetable peeler
- [ ] 3 large mixing bowls
- [ ] knife
- [ ] small bowl and whisk or fork
- [ ] food processor or box grater
- [ ] wooden mixing spoon
- [ ] large frying pan
- [ ] ladle
- [ ] fork
- [ ] pancake turner or spatula
- [ ] measuring spoons
- [ ] paper towels
- [ ] serving plate
- [ ] large microwave-safe bowl
- [ ] spatula or large spoon

Potato Latkes Ingredients:

- [ ] 4 potatoes
- [ ] 1 small onion
- [ ] 2 eggs
- [ ] 2 tablespoons matzo meal
- [ ] 1 teaspoon salt
- [ ] ⅛ teaspoon pepper
- [ ] vegetable oil

Strawberry Applesauce Ingredients:

- [ ] 16-ounce bag frozen strawberries
- [ ] 32-ounce jar applesauce

How to do it:

1. Use the vegetable peeler to peel the potatoes; place them into cold water in a large mixing bowl. With a knife, peel the onion and place it into the bowl.

2. Crack the eggs into the small bowl and stir them with the whisk.

3. Use the large hole attachment on your food processor to shred the potatoes and onion. Transfer to a mixing bowl. If using a box grater, grate the potatoes and onion over the mixing bowl against the large holes.

4. Take large scoops of potato mixture in your hands and squeeze out as much liquid as possible into the sink. Place the squeezed potato mixture into a mixing bowl.

5. Add the eggs, matzo meal, salt, and pepper to the potatoes and onions and mix with a wooden spoon until combined.

6. Pour about an inch of oil into the frying pan and place the frying pan over medium to high heat. Allow the oil to become very hot.

7. Ladle about a half-ladle of the mixture into the pan. Flatten with a fork and ladle in 3 to 5 more latkes. Do not place too close together. Fry for about 5 minutes; then flip with the pancake turner and fry for 2 minutes, until crispy but still soft on the inside.

8. Place 1–2 paper towels on a serving plate and transfer the fried latkes to the plate. Serve immedietely.

9. For strawberry applesauce: Place strawberries into a large microwave-safe bowl; microwave for 4–6 minutes, until mushy and juicy. Add the applesauce to the bowl and mix well with a spatula.

Estimated prep time: 20 minutes
Cooking time: 7 – 10 minutes per batch
Parve • Yield: 8 – 10 latkes

⋯ ⋯ sufganiot ⋯ ⋯

What you will need:

- [ ] medium bowl
- [ ] liquid measuring cup
- [ ] mixer with dough hook
- [ ] measuring cups and spoons
- [ ] clean dish towel
- [ ] pastry board
- [ ] rolling pin
- [ ] large round cookie cutter (2½" diameter), doughnut cutter, or drinking glass
- [ ] deep frying or candy thermometer
- [ ] large platter
- [ ] paper towels
- [ ] medium pot (approx. 6 quarts) or heavy frying pan
- [ ] slotted spoon, wide spatula, or pancake turner
- [ ] sugar sifter
- [ ] small knife, spoon, or pastry bag with large tip, optional

In Israel, around Chanukah time, it seems that sufganiot (doughnuts), are sold on every street corner. These delicacies are traditionally filled with jelly, but dulce de leche (caramel sauce) or custard filling taste yummy too. Nothing can compare to the taste of home-made doughnuts! Since there is hot oil involved, this project definitely requires adult supervision and involvement.

This recipe is from *What's Cooking: A Unique Collection of Kosher Recipes,* written by my friend Pessie Koplowitz; used by permission.

How to do it:

1. Place the warm water into the mixer bowl. Sprinkle the yeast and the one tablespoon sugar over the water. Let stand for 5-10 minutes or until the yeast mixture becomes foamy and bubbly.

2. Add the milk, sugar, salt, eggs, butter, and 2 cups flour. Mix on a low speed for a few minutes.

3. Beat in the remaining flour, ½ cup at a time, until the dough no longer sticks to the bowl. Knead for approximately 5 minutes or until the dough feels smooth and elastic.

4. Cover the dough with a dish towel and let rise in a warm place for 1 hour, or until doubled in size.

5. Sprinkle a counter or pastry board with a light coating of flour. Place the dough onto the floured surface and use a rolling pin to gently roll the dough to a ½" thickness.

6. Use the cookie cutter or the opening of the drinking glass to cut the dough into circles. Let rise again until doubled in size, approximately ½-hour. Re-roll scraps and cut more circles.

7. While the doughnut rounds are rising, clip a deep-frying thermometer to the side of the pot. Place 4 cups of oil into the pot and heat on medium-high heat until the temperature measures 375°F on the deep-frying thermometer.

8. Cover a platter with paper towels and set aside.

9. Carefully slide 4 doughnut rounds into the hot oil, using a slotted spoon or flat spatula. Let fry for about 40 seconds–1 minute, or until they rise to the surface of the oil. Turn over with the slotted spoon and fry for another 40 seconds–1 minute, or until golden brown.

Ingredients:

- ¼ cup warm water (105°-115°F)
- 2 (¼-oz.) packets dry yeast
- ¾ cup sugar plus 1 tablespoon
- 1½ cups milk, soy milk, or rice milk, at room temperature
- 1 teaspoon salt
- 2 eggs
- 6 tablespoons butter or margarine, softened
- 5-6 cups flour, plus more for pastry board
- 4 cups oil
- 1-2 cups confectioners' sugar, optional
- optional fillings: jelly, dulce de leche (caramel sauce), purchased custard filling

10. Remove the doughnuts from the oil and place on prepared platter.

11. Use the sugar sifter to sift the confectioners' sugar over the warm doughnuts.

Optional: Make a small slit in the side of each doughnut with a knife. Insert the jelly or other filling with a tablespoon. Or, fill a pastry bag with your filling of choice and insert the tip of the pastry bag into the opening. Pipe 1 tablespoon of filling into each doughnut.

Estimated prep time: 1 hour
Rising time: 1½ – 2 hours
Dairy or Parve • Yield: approximately 4 dozen sufganiot

TU B'SHEVAT

Just when you think it's going to be cold forever, Tu B'Shevat arrives and reminds us that spring is right around the corner. This day, the fifteenth day of the Jewish month of Shevat, is the "new year of trees," marking the season when the trees in Eretz Yisrael, the Land of Israel, begin to bud and blossom. The heavy winter rains taper off after laying the groundwork for bountiful crops to come. Spring is about to begin!

Tu B'Shevat is a lovely time for family and friends to get together and remember the bounty of Eretz Yisrael, especially the shivat haminim — the seven species of fruits indigenous to the land of Israel. What better way to do this than with one of Israel's most popular foods, the falafel, as the main dish? Add some veggies and dips, a stunning fruit centerpiece, and a luscious fruit buffet featuring many of the shivat haminim, and you've got a quick party that's guaranteed to melt the icicles and chase those storm clouds away.

So, if where you live the snow is falling and the wind-chill factor is heading down, down, down, you can still get a taste of the upcoming season by planting your own tree in a beautifully decorated pot. How exciting to see an avocado pit or citrus seed miraculously turn into a flourishing green plant — a harbinger of spring that is sure to come soon in your neck of the woods!

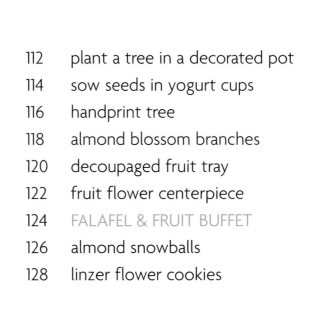

Many children plant trees on Tu B'Shevat in honor of the trees' "new year." You too can plant your very own tree using seeds found in fruit you have eaten, or by planting a bought citrus sapling.

plant a tree in a decorated pot

What you will need:

- ☐ 6"–7"-wide terra cotta pot with saucer
- ☐ acrylic paint, in the colors of your choice
- ☐ paintbrushes
- ☐ craft glue
- ☐ embellishments such as: seashells, buttons, flat marbles, rhinestones, ribbon, rickrack
- ☐ potting soil mix
- ☐ avocado pit, citrus fruit seeds, herb seeds, or citrus fruit sapling
- ☐ depending on plant: clear plastic cup, plastic wrap/ plastic food storage bag

How to do it:

1. Paint the pot and saucer with acrylic paint. Let dry. You may need to paint two coats for complete coverage. If so, allow for additional drying time between coats.

2. Decorate the pot by using craft glue to glue on seashells, buttons, marbles, rhinestones, ribbon, and/or rickrack. Let dry.

3. Fill pot almost to the top with potting soil. Plant seeds or sapling of your choice, following the instructions below.

Avocado Plant:

1. Wash any avocado flesh from the pit and let the pit dry for 24 hours. Peel the brown papery coating from the dry pit. It should slip off easily.

2. Place the pit, flat side down, ⅔ of the way into the soil. The pointy tip should be poking out of the soil.

3. Water well and cover the pot with a clear plastic cup so that it retains moisture. Water regularly. Remove the cup when the leaves begin to grow.

Citrus Seeds:

1. Place 2–3 seeds from a lemon, juice orange, tangerine, or lime into each pot. Push the seeds ½" down into the soil. Water well and place in a warm, sunny spot.

2. Cover the top of the plant with plastic wrap or place the pot into a plastic bag.

3. Water the plant only when the soil feels dry. Remove the plastic covering when a few leaves have formed on the stems.

4. After the stems have fully formed, pull out the weaker plants, leaving only one healthy plant in each pot. Continue to water when the soil feels dry. Keep in a sunny spot.

Citrus Sapling:

1. Remove the tree from the nursery pot and replant into your decorated pot, which should be one size larger than the nursery pot. Follow the instructions that come with the plant.

2. Water well. Keep the tree in a warm, sunny spot. The soil should always be moist, so water often.

Note: Most fruit plants grown from seed will not produce fruits. Rather, you will be rewarded for your effort with beautiful leaves and flowers.

Estimated time: 30 minutes – 1 hour (after avocado pit has dried for 24 hours)
Drying time: 1 – 2 hours

Although Tu B'Shevat is the "new year" of the trees, we found it fitting to do some planting of herb seeds at this time as well. Watch the results grow quickly. Remember to water the plants when the soil feels dry. Before you know it, you'll have herbs to add to your favorite salads. Just snip off the tops of the herbs when you need some — they'll grow back in no time.

sow seeds in yogurt cups

What you will need:

- ☐ empty yogurt or cottage cheese containers with covers
- ☐ hammer and large nail
- ☐ assorted acrylic paints suitable for plastic
- ☐ 1"- and ¼"-wide paintbrushes
- ☐ small stones
- ☐ shallow bowls or saucers, optional
- ☐ potting soil
- ☐ seeds such as: chives, parsley, basil, dill, or mint

How to do it:

1. Wash the containers and their covers very well and remove any paper labels. Dry.

2. Turn the containers over. Use the hammer and nail to make 2–3 holes in the bottom of each container.

3. Paint the outside of the containers and covers with acrylic paint. Allow to dry. Add designs using another paint color. Allow to dry.

4. Place several small stones in the bottom of each container. Fill the containers with soil and place the containers on the covers or in shallow bowls or saucers.

5. Read the directions on the seed packets. Sprinkle each type of seed into its own container and cover with soil, following the directions on the seed packet.

6. Place filled containers on a sunny windowsill or other sunny spot. Water lightly and keep the soil moist until the seeds start to grow.

Note: When the plants are 4 inches tall, and there is no chance of frost in the area where you live, you can put them outside in your garden. Transfer them to a larger pot or plant them directly in the soil.

Estimated time: 20 minutes – 30 minutes, divided
Drying time: 1 – 2 hours, divided

The Talmud tells us of a man who was walking in the desert. He was extremely tired, hungry, and thirsty. He found a shady fruit tree with a stream running alongside it. He ate the fruit of the tree, drank from the stream, and rested in the shade. He exclaimed, "Tree, tree, how can I bless you? If I were to bless you that your fruits should be sweet, they are already sweet. If I should bless you with pleasant shade, you already have shade. A stream already flows past you, so I can't bless you with water, either. I can only bless you that all the trees planted from your seeds should be just like you."

Craft this handprint family tree for your parents to illustrate that you hope your family will be blessed with the same blessing — that the children should be like the parents.

handprint tree

What you will need:

- [ ] scissors
- [ ] brown colored paper or scrapbook paper
- [ ] glue stick
- [ ] 1 (12"x12") sheet light blue heavy scrapbook paper or cardstock
- [ ] dark green and light green 12"x12" scrapbook paper or cardstock
- [ ] pencil
- [ ] gel pen or metallic marker
- [ ] ruler
- [ ] chipboard or sticker flowers

How to do it:

1. Using the scissors, cut the shape of a tree trunk from the brown paper. Glue the tree trunk to the center of the light blue paper.

2. Have each child place his or her hand, fingers spread out, on one of the green papers. Use a pencil to trace around the hand

3. Use the scissors to cut out each traced hand. With a glue stick, attach the hand cutouts over and around the top of the tree trunk (see photo).

4. With the gel pen, write the name of each child on his or her handprint. Write "Our Family" or your family's last name on the tree trunk.

5. Use the ruler to measure a 2"x12" piece of dark green scrapbook paper. Use the scissors to cut it out and cut slits into the paper. Don't cut all the way through to the end of the strip. Curl the ends against the scissor blade so that the strips resemble grass.

6. Glue the lower edge of the grass strip (below the slits) to the lower edge of the paper.

7. Cut thin strips of dark green paper for the flower stems. Glue stems behind grass. Attach a chipboard or sticker flower to the top of each stem.

Estimated time: 30 minutes

"The almond tree is budding,
And the sun is shining brightly,
Birds from every roof top,
Announce the arrival of the holiday"
(Israeli folk song)

In Israel, the "shkediah" (almond) is the first tree to begin budding around the time of Tu B'Shevat. By crafting these stunning almond blossom branches, you, too, can enjoy the sight of the flowering almonds, even if you don't live in Israel. They can almost be mistaken for the real thing. Use white tissue paper to mimic the blossoms of sweet almonds and pink tissue paper to resemble the bitter almond blossoms.

almond blossom branches

What you will need:

- [ ] 1 empty Pringles can (or similar-sized tubular container)
- [ ] 1 (12"x12") sheet of patterned scrapbook paper
- [ ] pencil
- [ ] scissors
- [ ] double-sided tape or glue lines/dots
- [ ] ruler
- [ ] 3–5 long branches
- [ ] 2 sheets of white and/or pink tissue paper
- [ ] green florist's tape or green masking tape

How to do it:

1. Wrap the paper around the empty container, overlapping the paper slightly. With a pencil, mark off measurements needed for the paper to completely cover the container and overlap a bit.

2. Use the scissors to cut the paper to size. Glue it to the container using double-sided tape or glue lines/dots.

3. Take the 2 sheets of tissue paper and place them one on top of the other. Use the ruler and pencil to measure and mark 1½"–2" squares on the paper. Use the scissors to cut out the squares. You will need at least 10 squares for each branch.

4. Place 1 square on top of another, rotating the top square so that the tissue papers look like an 8-pointed star. Pinch the squares in the middle and twist the middle into a point. It should start to look like a flower bud.

5. Wind floral tape around the pointed end of the paper blossom, and then wind the tape around a part of the branch until the flower is securely attached. Continue making blossoms and fastening them to branches until all the branches look like they are "in bloom" and you are pleased with the way they look.

6. Place the completed branches into the container.

Estimated time: 45 minutes

Serve fruits and nuts in style on Tu B'Shevat using this magnificent tray.
It is a work of art and can be displayed on a kitchen counter when not in use.

decoupaged fruit tray

What you will need:

- ☐ sandpaper
- ☐ unfinished wooden tray
- ☐ paper towels
- ☐ ½"- and 1½"-wide paintbrushes
- ☐ cream and beige colored acrylic paints (or colors of your choice)
- ☐ napkins or wrapping paper with fruit designs
- ☐ scissors
- ☐ decoupage medium, such as Mod Podge
- ☐ black or green felt, optional
- ☐ craft glue, optional

How to do it:

1. Use the sandpaper to sand down any rough edges on the tray. Wipe off wood dust with a damp paper towel.

2. Using the 1½" paintbrush, paint the entire tray with the cream paint. Allow to dry.

3. Take a dry ½" paintbrush and dab the bristles lightly in the beige paint. Brush the paint off against a paper towel to remove as much paint as possible. Lightly stroke the paint on to the tray to give it an antiqued look. Let dry.

4. While the tray is drying, cut out the fruit shapes from the napkins or wrapping paper.

5. Using a clean 1½" paintbrush, coat the inside of the dry tray with Mod Podge. Place the fruit shapes on the Mod Podge-covered surface. Smooth the shapes down carefully with your fingers. (It's okay if the shapes get a little wrinkly.) Allow to dry.

6. Brush another coat of Mod Podge on the entire inside of the tray, covering the cut-out shapes completely. Coat the raised sides of the tray, inside and out, as well. Allow to dry.

Optional: Cut a piece of felt the size of the underside of the tray. Use craft glue to glue the felt to the underside of the tray.

Note: Clean the tray only by wiping with a dry or slightly damp cloth.

Estimated time: 1 hour, divided
Drying time: 1–2 hours, divided

One of the campers' favorite workshops in Camp Hedvah is fruit decorating. The girls love to learn how to cut fresh fruit into beautiful shapes and display them in a mouth-watering manner. The best part of this activity is that you get to eat the "fruits of your labor" when you are done.

fruit flower centerpiece

What you will need:

- ☐ colander or strainer
- ☐ tray or large plate
- ☐ sharp knife and cutting board
- ☐ melon baller
- ☐ flower- and leaf-shaped cookie cutters
- ☐ wooden skewers
- ☐ small round cookie cutter
- ☐ some or all of the following fruits: pineapple, cantaloupe, honeydew, kiwis, red and green grapes, watermelon, strawberries

How to do it:

1. Place the colander in the sink and put the strawberries, kiwis, and grapes into it. Wash them very well.

2. Reserve one cantaloupe or honeydew for the basket. Peel all the rest of the fruits (except for the grapes). Remove any pits.

3. Cut the reserved melon in half. Remove a thin (½"-thick) slice from the bottom of the melon to keep the melon from rocking. Place the melon on the tray.

4. Use the melon baller to make balls from the reserved half-melon and half of the other cantaloupe or honeydew. Reserve the melon balls.

5. Cut as many 1-inch-thick slices as possible from the pineapple, watermelon, and the remaining honeydew and cantaloupe.

6. With the flower- and leaf-shaped cookie cutters, cut out fruit flowers and leaves from the pineapple and melons. Use a small round cookie cutter to cut a hole in the center of some of the fruit flowers. Place a melon ball into the opening of each cutout.

7. For each flower, poke the pointed end of a skewer through the flower shape, including the melon ball center, if applicable (see photo). Thread a leaf or several leaves onto the skewer under the flower. Stick the completed flower into the melon on the tray.

8. Thread strawberries and kiwi slices onto skewers. Thread 3–6 grapes onto each skewer.

9. Place skewers into the melon basket to form a pleasing arrangement.

Estimated time: 45 minutes • Parve

FALAFEL & FRUIT BUFFET

During the winter doldrums, a party that hints at spring to come is just the thing to perk up everyone's spirits. This Tu B'Shevat party takes its inspiration from the land of Israel whose fruit — the shivat haminim — we celebrate on this day. Fittingly, this party features one of Israel's most popular foods — the falafel. For dessert, cut up fruits and place in clear glass bowls with sauces and toppings alongside. Home-baked linzer cookies and almond snowballs are a treat for the guests to nibble on, as well as to take home for an after-the-party treat.

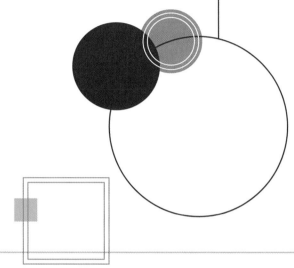

■ Set up:

Using two tables, one with the falafel components and one for dessert, is ideal for this buffet party. Have stacks of plates, napkins, and forks available near the food so that everyone can serve themselves easily. Make sure there are drinks and cups available as well.

■ Food:

Prepare frozen falafel balls according to package directions. (Or use falafel balls purchased from your local pizza store.) Place on a large platter and serve with pita breads cut in half and placed in a large basket. Fill bowls with cut-up vegetables, lettuce, sauerkraut, sliced pickles, and purchased tehina and hummus.

For drinks, skip the usual soda and serve Israeli fruit nectars and warm apple cider with cinnamon sticks.

For the fruit dessert, wash and/or peel assorted fruits, melons, and berries. Cut them into chunks and place in large bowls. Place honey-yogurt sauce (page 206), pomegranate syrup (page 42), purchased caramel sauce, and purchased chocolate sauce into small bowls.

Pour cocoa, confectioners' sugar, and cinnamon into clean spice shakers so that guests can sprinkle them on their choice of fruit.

Arrange almond snowballs (page 126) and linzer cookies (page 128) on serving platters or trays.

Estimated set up time: 1 hour

•••••••• almond snowballs ••••••••

What you will need:

- [ ] 2 cookie sheets
- [ ] parchment paper
- [ ] electric mixer
- [ ] measuring cups and spoons
- [ ] spatula
- [ ] small bowl
- [ ] wire baking rack

Ingredients:

- [ ] 1 cup (2 sticks) butter or margarine
- [ ] ½ cup confectioners' sugar
- [ ] 1 cup ground blanched almonds
- [ ] 1 tablespoon vanilla
- [ ] 2¼ cups flour
- [ ] coating: 1 cup confectioners' sugar

While the almond trees may start to bloom in Israel around Tu B'Shevat time, in the American northeast, where we live, it's hard to believe that spring is just around the corner. After spending time outside in the cold and snow it's nice to come in and warm up with a yummy "snowball" and a cup of hot cocoa.

How to do it:

1. Preheat oven to 350°F. Line cookie sheets with parchment paper. Set aside.

2. Place the butter into the bowl of the mixer and beat until light and fluffy. Add the ½ cup confectioners' sugar and mix to combine.

3. Add the ground almonds and vanilla; continue to mix the batter on low while slowly adding the flour. Turn mixer to high and mix, scraping down the sides of the bowl with a spatula as needed, until a soft dough forms.

4. Shape the dough into walnut-sized balls and place ½" apart on the prepared cookie sheets.

5. Place into hot oven and bake for 15 minutes. Remove from oven.

6. Place 1 cup confectioners' sugar into a small bowl. Roll the warm cookies, one at a time, in the bowl of confectioners' sugar. Place the sugar-coated cookies on the wire rack to cool.

Estimated prep time: 30 minutes
Bake time: 15 minutes
Dairy or Parve • Yield: approximately 5 dozen cookies

········ linzer flower cookies ········

What you will need:

- [ ] 2 cookie sheets
- [ ] parchment paper
- [ ] large bowl
- [ ] electric mixer
- [ ] measuring cups and spoons
- [ ] spatula
- [ ] 2 ziplock bags
- [ ] rolling pin
- [ ] teaspoon
- [ ] large round scalloped cookie cutter
- [ ] small (½") flower-shaped or round cookie cutter
- [ ] small sifter

Ingredients:

- [ ] 2 cups flour
- [ ] 1 teaspoon cinnamon
- [ ] ¼ teaspoon salt
- [ ] 1 cup (2 sticks) butter or margarine
- [ ] ⅓ cup brown sugar
- [ ] ⅓ cup white sugar
- [ ] 1 tablespoon vanilla extract
- [ ] 2 egg yolks
- [ ] 1 cup ground toasted almonds or hazelnuts
- [ ] 1 cup confectioners' sugar
- [ ] raspberry jam

The linzer cookie usually stands out on any tray of assorted cookies. Its glistening red center and confectioners' sugar coating just beg to be eaten. After shaping, baking, filling, and assembling the cookies, pop one (or two) into your mouth, because they'll be gone in no time!

This recipe has quite a few steps, so you might want to save it for a "snow day" when you have time to spend in the kitchen.

How to do it:

1. Preheat oven to 350°F. Line cookie sheets with parchment paper. Set aside.

2. In a large mixing bowl, stir together flour, cinnamon, and salt. Set aside.

3. Place the butter or margarine into the bowl of a mixer and beat for 1 minute until creamy. Add sugars, vanilla, and egg yolks; mix together.

4. Add ground nuts and mix until smooth.

5. Add the flour mixture in slowly, beating until smooth.

6. Divide the dough in half and place into the ziplock bags. Freeze for 1 hour.

7. Roll out one piece of the dough, ¼"-thick. Using a round scalloped cookie cutter, cut out as many cookies as you can.

8. Use a small flower-shaped cookie cutter to cut out the center of half the cookies. Place cookies 1" apart on prepared cookie sheets. Reroll any scraps to cut out more cookies. Repeat with remaining dough.

9. Place cookie sheets into the hot oven and bake for 12 minutes until cookies are lightly browned. Remove from the oven and place on wire racks to cool.

10. Place confectioners' sugar into small sifter. Sift sugar on top of the cookies that have the centers cut out.

11. Spoon ½ teaspoon jam on top of the other cookies. Sandwich the cut-out and the jam-covered cookies together.

Estimated prep time: 30 minutes

Chill time: 1 hour

Bake time: 12 minutes

Decorating time: 20 minutes

Dairy or Parve • Yield: approximately 30 cookies

PURIM

There is nothing, absolutely nothing, quite like Purim! It's the Jewish holiday of happiness and rejoicing. We celebrate Esther and Mordechai's victory over Haman and all the (seemingly) hidden miracles that occurred to save the Jews of Persia, and ensure our people's victory over evil throughout the ages. Purim is a jam-packed holiday made for friendship and good cheer that starts with the reading of the Megillah — the scroll relaying the Purim story. Then it's on to more revelry with mishloach manot — gifts of food exchanged, matanot l'evyonim — charity for the poor, and a blowout dinner — the seudat mitzvah — to end the day.

There is also nothing, absolutely nothing, quite like crafting for Purim. The Purim custom to dress up to emphasize the masquerading of the true self is even more fun in a costume you've made on your own. Try a kingly cape, a Chassidic shtriemel, or a crown made for a princess. Or take to the sky with your butterfly wings. Candy and cupcake mishloach manot treats somehow taste even better if they come packaged in a beautifully decorated homemade canister or a craft-foam hamantash container.

Wouldn't it be great if Purim could last for more than one day? If we start preparing some crafts projects early, then the Purim joy and fun can stretch out for weeks and weeks!

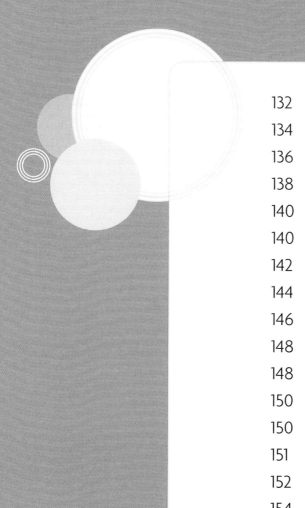

Drowning out Haman's name during the recitation
of the Megillah is done with relish by both kids and adults.
We use a colorful gragger (noisemaker) that does the job perfectly.

grand gragger

What you will need:

- [ ] self-adhesive or regular felt in assorted bright colors and/or patterns
- [ ] 1 small empty mixed-nuts container with lid (or similar-sized empty container with lid)
- [ ] pencil
- [ ] ruler or tape measure
- [ ] scissors
- [ ] craft glue
- [ ] jumbo or regular craft stick
- [ ] ½"-wide masking tape
- [ ] dry beans
- [ ] decorative-edge scissors
- [ ] assorted lengths of ribbons
- [ ] small jingle bells
- [ ] optional: sequins, pompoms, glitter

How to do it:

1. Wrap a piece of felt around the container. Use a pencil to mark the length and width of the container on the back of the piece of felt. Cut out. Trace the lid twice onto the back of the felt and cut out the felt circles.

2. Remove paper backing from the felt and press onto the can or glue non-adhesive felt to the outside of the can. Adhere a felt circle to the outside of the lid and to the bottom of the can.

3. With scissors, cut a small slit through the center of the lid and its felt cover. Push the craft stick through the slit so that half of the stick forms the handle. If it's loose, use masking tape to tape the top part of the craft stick to the inside of the lid.

4. Fill the can half-full with the dry beans. Cover the can with the lid. Be sure the stick is in securely. If it's still a bit wobbly, take off the lid and tape the stick more firmly to the inside of the lid and then replace the lid.

5. Use regular and decorative-edge scissors to cut strips of felt that fit around the can's circumference. Stick onto the gragger, taking care to cover the edge of the lid with felt.

6. Cut ribbons into 10" lengths and tie around the top of the handle. Tie bells to the ends of several ribbons.

Optional: Decorate the can by gluing on sequins, pompoms, glitter, and shapes cut from leftover felt.

Estimated time: 30 minutes

Put on a puppet show to entertain your family and friends during the festive Purim meal. You can get as creative as you want when decorating your basic puppets. Make as many of the Megillah's characters as you need for your puppet show.

purim puppets

What you will need:

- ☐ pencil
- ☐ scissors
- ☐ 2 large (9"x12") felt rectangles for each puppet
- ☐ cream or white felt
- ☐ craft glue, or glue gun and glue sticks
- ☐ decorative elements, including: yarn, buttons, lace, beads, pompoms, fabric scraps, pipe cleaners, googly eyes, fun fur, ribbons

How to do it:

1. Photocopy the puppet template (page 260) and cut out. Trace the template onto the back of two pieces of felt and cut out.

2. The second piece of felt that you cut out will be for the back of your puppet. Use your glue gun to carefully place a thin line of glue around the outer edge of the sides and top of the puppet. Press together to adhere front and back of puppet.

3. Cut a large circle from the cream-colored felt for the face and cut two small rounded triangles for the hands.

4. Use craft glue or glue gun and glue sticks to adhere the large round circle to the front of one puppet for the face. Glue the two triangles onto the hand area. Let dry.

5. Plan how you want to decorate your puppet: place the pompoms, googly eyes, yarn, and other materials on the puppet. When you are pleased with how it looks, glue the pieces to your puppet with craft glue or a glue gun and glue sticks. We used steps 1-3 of the crown craft on page 154 to make the puppets' crowns.

6. Glue decorative trim all along the front and back lower edge of the puppet.

Estimated time: 45 minutes

This hamantash looks good enough to eat.
Fill it with some yummy, edible ones.

mishloach manot large hamantash

What you will need:

- [ ] dinner plate
- [ ] 1 (12"x18") sheet of beige or brown craft foam
- [ ] pencil
- [ ] scissors
- [ ] hamentashen, food, or candy
- [ ] stapler
- [ ] purple tissue paper or cellophane paper
- [ ] 6"-7" plate, optional

How to do it:

1. Place the plate on the craft foam and trace around the plate.

2. Cut out the circle of craft foam. Place the hamantashen, food, or candy into the center of the circle.

3. To make the hamantash's triangular shape, lift up two sides of the circle and staple together on top, where the two sides meet. Lift up the remaining side and staple to each of the other sides (see photo).

4. Cut out a square of tissue paper or cellophane slightly larger than the hamantash's opening. Stuff the tissue paper or cellophane into the opening to cover the food.

Optional: Use a 6"-7" plate as your template to make a smaller hamantash (see photo).

Estimated time: 10 minutes

If you are dressing up as a clown this Purim, then this mishloach manot holder is the one for you. It ties in to the festive, jolly spirit of the day.

clown hat container

What you will need:

- ☐ pencil
- ☐ heavy 12"x12" scrapbook paper, cardstock, or oak tag
- ☐ scissors
- ☐ stapler
- ☐ large pompoms
- ☐ craft glue
- ☐ tape
- ☐ pompom trim, marabou trim, optional

How to do it:

1. Photocopy the hat template (page 261) and cut out. Trace the template onto the back of the paper of your choice.

2. Cut out the hat shape. Roll it into a cone and staple the overlapping edges.

3. Trace the hat's round opening onto another piece of paper and cut out the circle. Set aside.

4. Glue a large pompom to the top of the hat.

5. Fill the paper hat with treats. Tape the circle over the hat's opening.

Optional: Before filling it, trim the hat by gluing pompom fringe or marabou trim to the bottom edge.

Estimated time: 10 minutes

sweet treat

What you will need:

- [ ] 2 red 6" disposable plastic plates
- [ ] jumbo or regular craft stick
- [ ] treats
- [ ] stapler
- [ ] cellophane bag or cellophane paper
- [ ] curling ribbon

How to do it:

1. Staple the craft stick to the rim of one plate, leaving most of it to extend out of the plate.

2. Fill the plate with treats. Cover the filled plate with the second plate and staple around the rim to close.

3. Wrap the "lollipop" in cellophane and fasten it by tying curling ribbon around the stick. Fluff the cellophane out on the bottom, below the curling ribbon.

Estimated time: 5 minutes

dandy candy

What you will need:

- [ ] scissors
- [ ] paper towel roll tube
- [ ] tissue paper
- [ ] clear cellophane paper
- [ ] scotch tape
- [ ] 2 small rubber bands
- [ ] candy
- [ ] curling ribbon

How to do it:

1. With scissors, cut the tube in half horizontally. (Save the other tube half to make another "candy.")

2. Cut tissue paper and cellophane paper, making sheets 6 inches longer and a little bit wider than the tube.

3. Place the tissue paper onto the cellophane and place the tube at the edge, on top of the tissue. Tape the edge of the papers to the tube; roll the papers around the tube and tape the edge.

4. Knot a rubber band around one end to close one end of the tube. Fill the tube with candies and use a rubber band to close the other end.

5. Tie curling ribbon around the rubber bands.

Estimated time: 10 minutes

Make these pretty caddies to send to your friends near and far. Since they are made from cardboard containers, they will hold up well even if you have far to go to deliver them or are sending them through the mail.

(Instructions for Cute Caddy II can be found on page 144.)

cute caddy I

What you will need:

- ☐ clean round cardboard container (such as from breadcrumbs, nuts, or baby formula)
- ☐ craft glue
- ☐ colored jumbo or regular craft sticks
- ☐ ribbon
- ☐ decorative-edge scissors

How to do it:

1. Spread glue around the top and bottom outer edge of the container.
2. Glue the craft sticks around the entire container. Let dry.
3. Tie a ribbon around the center of the container and trim the ends with decorative-edge scissors.

Estimated time: 10 minutes
Drying time: 1 hour

cute caddy II

What you will need:

- [ ] patterned scrapbook paper
- [ ] clean round cardboard container, such as from breadcrumbs, nuts, or baby formula
- [ ] pencil
- [ ] scissors or paper cutter
- [ ] double-sided tape and/or glue lines or glue dots
- [ ] Phillips-head screwdriver or awl
- [ ] 1"-1½"-wide wire-edged ribbon
- [ ] decorative edge scissors
- [ ] rickrack, pompom trim, fringe, beaded trim, optional

How to do it:

1. Wrap the scrapbook paper around the container. On the plain side of the paper, use the pencil to mark the height of the container. Mark the width of the container plus one extra inch.

2. Cut out the paper using your scissors or paper cutter.

3. Place strips of double-sided tape or glue lines all around the container and stick the paper neatly onto the outer surface of the container.

4. Use the screwdriver to carefully poke a hole ½" down from the top of the container. Then poke another hole 1" under the first hole.

5. Repeat step 4 on the opposite side of the can.

6. Cut a 14" piece of wire-edged ribbon. Tie a knot near the end of the ribbon.

7. Thread the long piece of ribbon through a lower hole, leaving the knotted end on the outside of the container. Poke the long piece of ribbon through the upper hole. Bring the ribbon over the top of the container and poke the ribbon through the upper hole from the outside, on the other side of the container, leaving 4" for slack. This will form your handle. Poke the ribbon through the last lower hole and tie the remaining piece into a knot. Trim the knotted ends if necessary.

8. Trace the cover of the container onto a piece of scrapbook paper. Cut out the circle with decorative edge scissors so that the circle will be slightly smaller than the cover of the container. Tape the circle to the cover with double-sided tape.

Optional: Trim the container with the decorative trim of your choice.

Estimated time: 15 minutes

PURIM TIPS

- Place heavier items on the bottom of the basket or container and lighter items on top.

- Make sure the container is sturdy enough to hold heavy items or glass bottles/jars.

- If you are sending home-baked goods, be sure to write a label with the ingredients' kosher certification and possible allergenic ingredients, such as nuts.

- Always put a label with your name on the mishloach manot so that the recipient will know who sent it.

- If you are sending baked goods through the mail, be sure to send sturdy items such as brownies and/or cookies that are not too fragile. Make sure to wrap the baked goods well in plastic wrap or foil. Place bubble wrap or crumpled newspaper between the wrapped goodies and the sides of the box.

- Mail mishloach manot a week before Purim so that they will arrive on time.

- When delivering mishloach manot in your neighborhood, be sure to look both ways before crossing the street.

- Make sure your costume is comfortable so that you can move about easily. There should not be extra material to trip you.

Dressing up on Purim is so much fun and something most children look forward to the entire year. Use the instructions on the following pages to create an array of hats and accessories to enhance a variety of costumes.

In the time it takes to say "abracadabra" (okay, just a bit longer than that) you can craft a cape worthy of any good king, queen, or "magician." The most incredible part is that it's done with no needle and thread involved. How's that for a Purim miracle!

cool cape

What you will need:

- ☐ 36"x36" piece of felt (sold in packages in most craft stores)
- ☐ tape measure
- ☐ straight pins
- ☐ sharp scissors
- ☐ 48" length of 1"-2" wide ribbon
- ☐ 4 yards 1" wide rickrack or 2-4 yards marabou or fake fur trim
- ☐ fabric glue, or glue gun and glue sticks

How to do it:

1. Place the felt onto a flat surface. On one side of the felt square, measure and fold over a 5"x36" section. Pin the folded section to the remaining felt with straight pins, to hold in place.

2. Use the sharp scissors to cut 1" slits into the folded felt: cut 20 slits spaced approximately 2" apart.

3. Remove the pins and unfold the felt. There will be 2" slits. Weave the ribbon through the slits. The part that folds over will form the collar of the cape.

4. Cut a length of approximately 50"-52" of rickrack or marabou to fit around the outer edge of the collar of the cape. Use fabric glue or glue gun and glue sticks to attach the rickrack to the edge of the collar. Fold the rickrack at a 45° angle when you reach a corner and continue gluing.

5. Turn the cape over and hot glue the rest of the rickrack around the edge of the cape, not including the collar area. (When the cape is worn the collar will be folded down.)

Note: This cape will fit a 4-8-year-old child. To make the cape longer or shorter using this size piece of felt, increase or decrease the length of the collar. These instructions can also easily be adapted for a larger piece of material.

Estimated time: 15 minutes

shtriemel

- ☐ 2 (12"x15") pieces of brown fake fur
- ☐ glue gun and glue sticks
- ☐ scissors
- ☐ 1 large black velvet kippa

How to do it:

1. Lay one piece of fake fur, fur side down, on a table. Fold one-third (4") of the fur up toward the middle.

2. Apply hot glue to the unfolded section. Fold the unglued section onto the glued area. Press to form a flat tube shape.

3. Repeat with the second piece of fur. Glue the tubes together at one end. Measure the fur tube around head and trim off extra fabric.

4. Glue the two ends together to form a circle. Place the kippa into the fur circle. Hot glue the edges of the kippa to the fur inside the circle.

Estimated time: 20 – 30 minutes

medieval princess hat

What you will need:

- ☐ 1 large sheet of craft foam or oak tag
- ☐ clothespins
- ☐ scissors
- ☐ stapler
- ☐ feather boa, crepe paper streamers, or tulle
- ☐ masking tape
- ☐ measuring tape
- ☐ thin elastic or narrow ribbon
- ☐ glitter, rhinestones, ribbons, and trim, optional

How to do it:

1. Roll the craft foam into a cone and hold it together with clothespins. Measure to see if it fits and adjust the clothespins. With the scissors, trim the ends so that the base is level.

2. Staple the hat together at the lower edge and tape the seam on the inside. Remove the clothespins.

3. Place the end of feather boa, crepe paper streamers, or tulle into the small opening at the top and tape or staple to inside of hat.

4. With the tape measure, measure child's face from ear to ear, going under the chin. Cut thin elastic 1" longer than the measured length. Or, use 2 lengths of ribbon and tie under the chin.

5. Staple one end of the thin elastic or a ribbon to the inside of hat. Staple the other end of the elastic or a ribbon to the opposite side of hat.

Optional: Decorate the hat with glitter, rhinestones, ribbons, and trim.

Estimated time: 15 minutes

crown

What you will need:

- ☐ scissors
- ☐ pencil
- ☐ metallic poster board
- ☐ white glue
- ☐ gold or silver glitter
- ☐ sequins or rhinestones
- ☐ stapler

How to do it:

1. Photocopy the crown template (page 260) and cut out. Trace the template onto the back of the poster board 6–8 times (depending on size needed), side-by-side, so that a long crown form is outlined.

2. Cut out the crown. Decorate the crown by gluing glitter, sequins, and/or rhinestones on (see photo on page 147). Let dry.

3. Measure the crown on your head. Staple the overlapping ends together; trim if necessary.

Estimated time: 10 – 15 minutes

glittery mask

What you will need:

- ☐ plastic eye mask
- ☐ paper plate
- ☐ white glue or glittering glue
- ☐ glitter

How to do it:

1. Place the mask onto a paper plate. Coat the mask with a thin layer of glue.

2. Sprinkle glitter all over the mask and shake off the excess glitter (see photo on page 147). Let dry.

Estimated time: 5 minutes

Drying time: 30 minutes – 1 hour

When my daughter was six, she had her heart set on being a butterfly for Purim. Since this "big decision" was made very close to Purim, we didn't have time to order the butterfly wings from a catalog. Examining the picture, I noticed that the filmy material of the wings looked like nylon stockings! I improvised this version, which surpassed those in the catalog. The wings (see following page) were such a hit they were even lent out the next year to my friend's daughter and they are now a treasured item in my kids' dress-up box.

butterfly antennae

What you will need:

- ☐ glue gun and glue sticks
- ☐ 2 large pompoms
- ☐ 2 pipe cleaners
- ☐ pink marabou
- ☐ 1"-wide plastic hair band
- ☐ scissors

How to do it:

1. Use the glue gun and glue sticks to attach one pompom to each pipe cleaner. Curl each pipe cleaner around your finger to give it a coiled look. Set aside.

2. Hot glue a strip of marabou to the headband. Trim the ends. Wrap one end of an antenna around the headband near the center; twist to secure in place. Repeat on the other side of the headband with the second antenna.

Estimated time: 5 minutes

butterfly wings

What you will need:

- [ ] 3 wire hangers
- [ ] duct tape
- [ ] scissors
- [ ] 2 pairs queen-size white or pink pantyhose
- [ ] twist ties
- [ ] needle and thread or safety pin
- [ ] 2 yards (⅜"-wide) white braided elastic
- [ ] white glue or glittering glue
- [ ] glitter
- [ ] glue gun and glue sticks, optional
- [ ] pink marabou, ribbons, silk flowers, optional

How to do it:

1. Take one hanger and bend it into a triangular-oval shape. Bend in the hook part so that it forms a small oval loop.

2. Take the second hanger and shape it to match the first hanger. Put the hook of the second hanger through the small loop of the first hanger; bend the hook to secure. This will form the top part of the butterfly wings.

3. Take the third hanger and bend the bottom part at the center up to the hook on top. Bend the two sides to form two small wings.

4. Bend the hook of the third hanger around the hooks of the other wings; the small lower wings will slightly overlap the top two.

5. Wrap duct tape around the hooks in the center to secure the wings. Use lots of duct tape so that the wings will be attached well and so that the wire hooks are covered completely and won't poke out.

6. Cut the legs off both pairs of pantyhose. Stretch a cut leg over one lower wing. Secure with a twist tie and trim the extra with a scissor. Repeat on the second lower wing.

7. Stretch another pantyhose leg over each top wing. Secure with a twist tie but don't cut off the excess pantyhose. Loop the excess around the duct-taped middle and stitch it in place, or pin it together tightly with a safety pin to cover tape completely.

8. Cut the elastic in half. Knot the two ends of each elastic piece together to form two loops of elastic. Stitch or pin each loop to the inside of the center of the wings. Try the wings on by placing the wings like a backpack over child's shoulders. If the elastic is very loose, open knots and tie them tighter. Trim off any excess elastic.

9. Use glue to "draw" swirls and/or designs on the wings. Shake glitter over the wet glue. Shake off any excess glitter and let the wings dry. Optional: Use glue gun to attach marabou around the wing frame and center. You can also add ribbons and silk flowers to decorate the center.

Estimated time: 1 hour

Drying time: 1–2 hours

Tie the dress-up theme into you Purim Seudah by using royal napkin rings and dramatic place cards at each place setting.

crown napkin ring

What you will need:

- ☐ scissors
- ☐ pencil
- ☐ metallic cardstock
- ☐ glittering glue, sequins, rhinestones, optional
- ☐ permanent marker or paint marker, optional
- ☐ cellophane tape
- ☐ 3" strip narrow elastic

How to do it:

1. For each crown napkin ring: Photocopy the mini crown template (page 255) and cut out.

2. Trace the template onto the back of the cardstock and cut out.

3. If you like, you can decorate the crown with glittering glue, sequins, and or rhinestones. Let dry. Use the marker to write your guest's name on the crown.

4. Tape elastic to the back of the crown, ½" from each end.

Estimated time: 10 minutes

mask place card

What you will need:

- ☐ scissors
- ☐ pencil
- ☐ metallic cardstock
- ☐ metallic paint marker
- ☐ cellophane tape
- ☐ small skewers

How to do it:

1. For each place card: Photocopy the mask template (page 255) and cut out.

2. Trace the template onto the back of the cardstock and cut out.

3. Use the paint marker to personalize with your guest's name. Turn over and tape the top of the skewer to the side of the mask.

Estimated time: 10 minutes

PURIM MASQUERADE PARTY

Hosting a Purim dress-up party is so much fun! Invite your friends over for an exciting, lively party filled with music, dancing, and good cheer. Purim night after the Megillah reading is a great time for this party, but if that doesn't work for you, then any day or night close to Purim is a good time for everyone to gather to get into the Purim spirit.

A party like this should not be difficult to set up, especially if it is being held on a school/work day, when you don't have time to spare for minor details.

■ Set up:

To make room for dancing and games, push all the furniture in the room to one side, or move it to other rooms. Place one or two long tables and one small table at the side of the room and drape colorful tablecloths or sheets over them. Place food on bright-colored trays and put out lots of plates and napkins. Set out drinks on the small table.

For a cute as well as practical centerpiece, place a row of clean buckets, clear jars, or mini pails down the table. Fill each with one color and/or type of candy, such as jelly beans, lollipops, and chocolate lentils. You can tie helium balloons to the handle of each bucket. Have a stack of paper bags or small buckets on hand so that at the end of the party each guest can fill them from the centerpiece containers.

■ Food:

The party food should be as much fun to look at as it is to eat! So make it miniature! Serve bite-sized food with decorative toothpicks, eliminating forks and knives.

Serve trays of mini beef burgers (page 158), "franks in blanks," mini potato knishes, mini egg rolls, and burekas. Set out small bowls of ketchup, mustard, and duck sauce.

Make sandwiches with soft white or whole wheat bread and your favorite deli meats. Use small cookie cutters to cut the sandwiches into shapes.

Serve baby corn, baby carrots, grape tomatoes, sugar snap peas, and small peppers with the dip of your choice.

Bake shoestring French fries according to package directions. Serve in paper cups or in clown hat containers (page 138) placed in a cupcake stand.

For dessert, serve mini cupcakes, hamantashen (page 159), and sorbet (page 189) in mini trifle cups. You can also make mini fruit kabobs for a healthy and light end to your meal. Use a melon baller to make balls of watermelon, honeydew, and cantaloupe; then place one of each on a toothpick or small skewer.

mini beef burgers

These miniature burgers are so juicy, they will be gone in a bite or two; so double (or triple!) the recipe if you're expecting a lot of guests. Serve them in mini cocktail or dinner rolls. If you can't find such small rolls, take regular rolls and use a 2" biscuit cutter to cut them down to size. Save the leftover roll pieces to make breadcrumbs.

What you will need:

- [ ] large bowl
- [ ] measuring spoons
- [ ] spatula or mixing spoon
- [ ] broiler pan or grill pan
- [ ] slotted spoon

Ingredients:

- [ ] 1 pound ground beef
- [ ] 1 tablespoon barbeque sauce
- [ ] 1 teaspoon salt
- [ ] ½ teaspoon pepper
- [ ] 1 dozen cocktail or dinner rolls
- [ ] optional garnishes: cherry tomato, pickle, lettuce

How to do it:

1. Preheat the oven to broil. Place all the ingredients into the large bowl. Use the spatula or your hands to mix the ground beef with the sauce and salt and pepper.

2. Roll the mixture into 12 (2") balls; then flatten to ½" thick patties and place them, 1" apart, onto a broiler pan.

3. Place them into the oven set on broil. (Or, coat a grill pan with a thin coat of oil and place grill pan over high heat. Use a slotted spoon to slide the burgers onto the preheated grill pan.)

4. Broil or grill the burgers for 3-5 minutes (If using a grill pan, after 2 minutes flip burgers over to grill the other side.)

5. Remove from the oven and use a slotted spoon to transfer the burgers to a platter.

6. Place the burgers into mini rolls (see photo, page 157) and garnish with a slice of cherry tomato, pickle, and piece of lettuce if you wish.

Estimated prep time: 15 minutes
Cook time: 5 minutes
Meat • Yield: 12 burgers

·······• easy hamantashen •·······

When my friend Mindy heard that I was writing a craft and recipe book, she graciously shared her Bubby's famous hamantash recipe with me. This dough produces a lot of hamantashen, so you'll have enough for your family as well as for sending in your mishloach manot packages.

What you will need:

- [ ] electric mixer
- [ ] knife
- [ ] measuring cup and spoons
- [ ] liquid measuring cup
- [ ] pastry board
- [ ] rolling pin
- [ ] drinking glass
- [ ] cookie sheets
- [ ] spatula
- [ ] wire rack

Ingredients:

- [ ] 1½ cups margarine, softened
- [ ] 3 cups sugar
- [ ] 6 eggs
- [ ] 1 cup orange juice
- [ ] 7 cups flour
- [ ] 3 teaspoons baking powder
- [ ] 1 teaspoon salt
- [ ] Fillings: apricot, prune, poppy, strawberry, or raspberry jam; chocolate chips

How to do it:

1. Cut the margarine into chunks and place into the mixer bowl. Add the sugar; then cream together on a medium-high setting.

2. When the mixture is light and fluffy, turn mixer to low and add the eggs, one at a time, and orange juice. Mix to combine.

3. Change the beater for the dough hook. Set the mixer to low. Slowly add the flour, baking powder, and salt. Mix until it becomes a soft dough.

4. Preheat the oven to 350°F. Sprinkle part of a clean counter or a pastry board with flour. Divide the dough into 3 parts and roll each ⅓" thick. Place one piece of dough on the floured surface. Roll out into a large rectangle. If the dough is too sticky to work with, sprinkle the rolling pin and dough with a bit of flour.

5. Use the drinking glass to cut circles from the dough. Reroll any scraps and cut out more circles.

6. Place a half-teaspoon of filling into the center of each circle. To form a hamantash, fold two edges to the middle and pinch together. Fold up the remaining section and pinch together. (See photo on page 136).

7. Place the hamantashen, 1" apart, on the cookie sheets. Bake for 12–15 minutes or until they just start to turn golden brown on the bottom.

8. Use a spatula to transfer the hamantashen to a wire rack to cool.

Estimated prep time: 30 minutes – 45 minutes

Bake time: 12 – 15 minutes

Parve • Yield: approximately 4 dozen hamantashen

purim pops

- ☐ cookie sheets
- ☐ parchment paper
- ☐ cookie sticks or lollipop sticks
- ☐ wire rack
- ☐ small bowls
- ☐ spatula

Ingredients:

- ☐ 1 package or roll frozen sugar cookie dough (or make your favorite slice-and-bake cookie dough)
- ☐ decorations such as: cereal, mini chocolate chips, red hots, candy corn, colored sprinkles, silver dragees, nuts, jelly beans, hamantashen, gum balls
- ☐ 1 container dairy or parve vanilla frosting (or make a bowl of your favorite vanilla frosting)

These cookie pops are so much fun to decorate. All your friends will get a kick out of your cute creations. Let your imagination go wild!

How to do it:

1. Take the cookie dough out of the freezer and let it defrost for 15 minutes. Preheat oven to 350°F. Line cookie sheets with parchment paper.

2. Slice the cookie dough into ½"-thick circles and place them 1" apart on the cookie sheets. Insert a cookie stick into each dough circle. Bake the cookies according to directions on the package.

3. Take cookie pops out of the oven and place on a wire rack to cool.

4. Place the decorating candies and cereal into small bowls.

5. Use a spatula to spread vanilla icing on each cookie pop. Put an extra blob of icing on the top as the base for a hamantash hat, if desired. Decorate the pops in any way that you wish, using some or all of the suggested decorative elements.

Estimated prep time: 15 minutes
Bake time: approximately 12 minutes
Cooling time: 30 minutes
Decorating time: 30 minutes
Dairy or Parve • Yield: will vary

PESACH

The sun has majestically set, the home gleams, and the table is set with the finest china, crystal, and silver. The children wait, wide-eyed, for the Pesach seder that is about to begin!

Pesach, or Passover, is the festival with the strongest orientation toward family. From parent to child, from generation to generation, the messages of freedom, liberation, and our national destiny are transmitted. At the seder, we retell the fascinating and miraculous story of the Jewish Exodus from Egypt. Children ask the questions; adults provide the answers they heard when they were children themselves.

There's cleaning and preparing to be done before Pesach. Our homes must be free of all "chametz," leavened foods, before the holiday begins. Ridding the home of chametz can consume the time, effort, and energy of the entire family, and loving bonds may become a bit frayed. Here's where holiday crafting can work its magic. It's wonderful — and important — to take a break and create a family crafts project. Forty-five minutes can result in a gorgeous seder plate and still leave time to scrub the fridge! Look ahead to family activities you'll be sharing, and fashion a travel pack for holiday trips. These moments will lay the groundwork to ensure that the holiday itself is "oh so special."

As always, a family crafts project helps us enjoy some precious family time — even when time is precious.

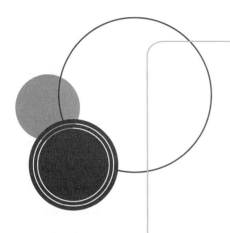

Before cleaning for Pesach, create a family checklist and post it in a prominent place. Everyone will know what was done and which tasks are still available.

In the *Olomeinu, Our World*, magazine, a reader from Belgium described a Prize Box that keeps chores fun and exciting. My family's "Prize Box" is filled with slips of paper with rewards written on them. After completing a Pesach-related chore, a child picks a reward, varying from staying up a half-hour past bedtime to a Slurpee or a small toy.

"cleaning for pesach" checklist

What you will need:

- ☐ 1 (8½"x11") sheet cardstock or heavy paper
- ☐ markers, optional
- ☐ scissors and glue
- ☐ ruler and pencil
- ☐ 1 (12"x12") sheet patterned scrapbook paper
- ☐ peel-and-stick magnetic tape

How to do it:

1. Photocopy the Pesach checklist template (page 263) onto cardstock or heavy paper. Or, create your own checklist. Decorate with markers if you wish.

2. Use the ruler and pencil to measure and draw a 9"x11½" rectangle on the scrapbook paper. With scissors, cut out the rectangle. Glue the checklist to the scrapbook paper.

3. Cut two pieces of magnetic tape and attach them to the top and bottom of the back of the scrapbook paper.

Estimated time: 10 minutes

prize box

What you will need:

- ☐ ruler and pencil
- ☐ 1 (12"x12") sheet patterned scrapbook paper
- ☐ small tin or box
- ☐ scissors
- ☐ scrap of white paper to fit the front of the box
- ☐ tape runner or double-sided tape
- ☐ alphabet stickers
- ☐ brown inkpad, optional

How to do it:

1. Measure, mark, and cut a strip of scrapbook paper to fit around the tin. Attach strip to the tin with tape runner or double-sided tape.

2. Place the tin's lid, face down, on the remaining paper. Trace around the lid. Cut out the traced shape and attach to the top.

3. Cut out a rectangle of white paper to fit on the front of the tin. Decorate it with stickers spelling out the words "Prize Box."

4. Use tape runner or double-sided tape to attach the white rectangle to the center of the tin.

Optional: After cutting out the white paper rectangle, rub a brown ink pad lightly around the edges.

Estimated time: 15 minutes

CLEANING FOR PESACH CHECKLIST

LIVING ROOM/FAMILY ROOM
- ☐ Couch
- ☐ Chairs
- ☐ Side table(s)
- ☐ Coffee table
- ☑ Cabinets/bookshelves
- ☐ Books and games
- ☐ _____

DINING ROOM
- ☐ Table
- ☐ Chairs
- ☐ Buffet/sideboard
- ☐ Cabinetry
- ☐ Serving ware
- ☐ _____
- ☐ _____

KITCHEN
- ☐ Table
- ☐ Chairs
- ☐ Cabinets and drawers
- ☐ Pantry
- ☐ Dishes
- ☐ Flatware and cutlery
- ☐ Pots and pans
- ☐ Mixer
- ☐ Food processor
- ☐ Toaster
- ☐ Oven
- ☐ Stove
- ☐ Microwave
- ☐ Refrigerator and freezer
- ☐ Sinks
- ☐ Dish washer
- ☐ Garbage disposal
- _____

BEDROOM(S)
- ☑ Bed
- ☑ Closet
- ☑ Night table
- ☐ Under the bed
- ☐ Desk
- ☐ Dresser drawers
- ☐ Bookshelf and books
- ☐ Wastebasket
- ☐ _____
- ☐ _____

BATHROOM(S)
- ☐ Vanity
- ☐ Medicine cabinet
- ☐ Wastebasket
- ☐ _____

PLAYROOM
- ☐ Toy box
- ☐ Closet and sheves
- ☐ Toys
- ☑ Games and puzzles
- ☑ Table and chairs
- ☐ _____
- ☐ _____

GARAGE
- ☐ Car
- ☐ Car seat
- ☐ Stroller
- ☐ Outdoor toys

MISCELLANEOUS
- ☐ Pocketbooks and purses
- ☐ Backpacks and briefcases
- ☐ Telephones and computer(s)
- ☐ Vacuum cleaner and brooms
- ☐ Garbage cans

prize box

from toy

from chores

For many people, celebrating Pesach means getting together with family that lives far away. If you're traveling or visiting relatives, put together this travel pack to make the car ride or plane trip more enjoyable. Kids will be so busy using the stuff in the pack, they won't have time to bicker or to keep saying, "Are we there yet?"

hit-the-road travel pack

What you will need:

☐ backpack or tote bag

☐ paperback book(s)

☐ crayons and coloring books

☐ travel-size game or felt board game

☐ deck of cards/card games

Trail Mix:

☐ raisins, nuts, chocolate chips, dried fruit

How to do it:

1. Fill the backpack with some or all of the listed materials, or craft the notepad below and include it in the travel pack. These are just suggestions; take along anything that will capture kids' interest and that doesn't take up too much space or have many pieces that might get lost in the car.

2. Make trail mix to munch on. Place an ample amount of raisins, nuts, chocolate chips, and dried fruit in a ziplock bag. Store in the backpack.

Estimated time: 10 minutes

hit-the-road travel notepad

What you will need:

☐ medium-sized spiral-bound pad of paper

☐ 1 (8½"x11") sheet cardstock

☐ pencil

☐ scissors or paper cutter

☐ glue stick or tape runner

☐ large paper tag

☐ alphabet stickers

☐ 15" length of ½"-wide ribbon

How to do it:

1. Trace the front of the pad onto the back of the cardstock and cut out.

2. Glue the cardstock rectangle to the cover of the notepad

3. Cut a 3" piece of ribbon and knot through the tag's hole. Stick letters spelling "Trip Notes" onto the tag. Use the glue stick or tape runner to glue the tag to the center of the notepad.

4. Tie one end of the remaining ribbon to a pen or pencil and the other end to the spiral binding of the notepad.

Estimated time: 15 minutes

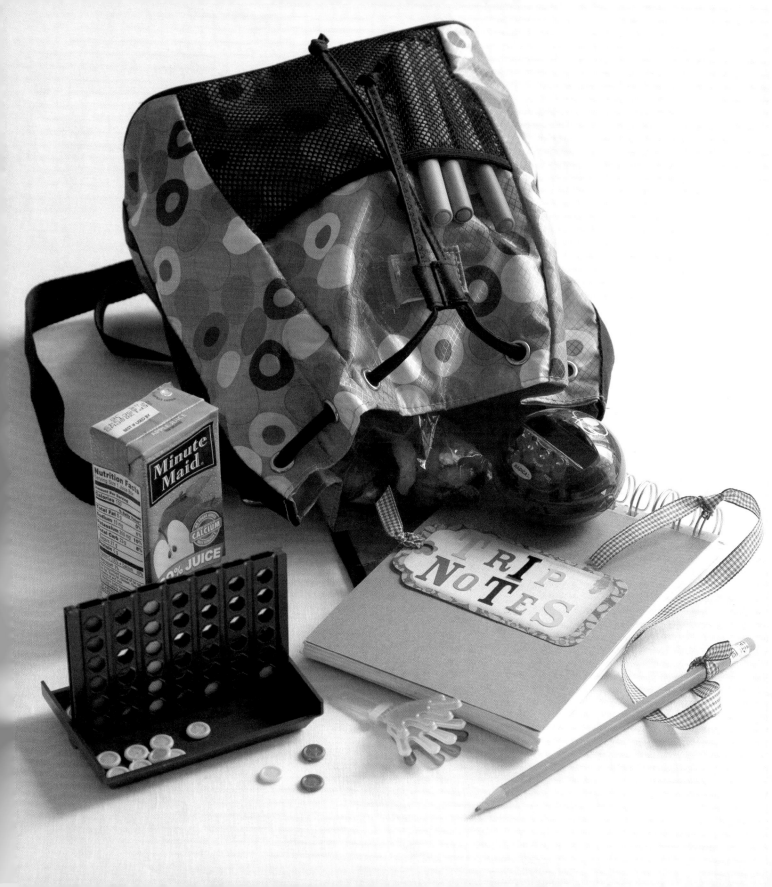

The ke'ara (seder plate) holds pride of place at the seder table. This plate holds the symbolic foods used during the seder. In many homes the ke'ara is a family heirloom, lovingly taken out every year for the seder. For those starting their own seder traditions, or if you'd like to provide guests with their own seder plates, this craft is for you. Here's your chance to create your own modern-day heirloom.

seder plate

What you will need:

- ☐ glass charger or serving plate
- ☐ 5-lb. bag of sea glass pieces, found in the floral decorating section of craft stores and WalMart
- ☐ E6000 adhesive
- ☐ paper towel
- ☐ small plates or bowls

How to do it:

1. Working with a 2-inch section at a time, spread a thin layer of glue on the plate's upper rim. Glue down the glass shards, fitting them together in an artistic pattern. Continue gluing on more pieces in the same manner until the rim is completely covered. You will need to hold down the glass for a few seconds so that the pieces don't slide around.

2. For a second layer, spread a small amount of glue on the back of each piece and attach it to the top of the first layer. You can add as many layers as you like in the same manner.

3. Clean up any glue drips with a damp paper towel. (The glue gums up and can be pulled off easily.) Let dry for at least 24 hours before using.

4. Place small plates or bowls onto your seder plate to hold the symbolic foods.

Note: Hand-wash after use.

Estimated time: 30 minutes – 45 minutes
Drying time: at least 24 hours

Eastern European (Ashkenazi) Charoset

At the seder we dip the marror into charoset to remind us of the mortar used by the Jews when they were slaves in Egypt. Here is a charoset recipe originating from Eastern Europe.

Peel 1 large apple and chop or grate it into a small bowl. Mix in ¾ cup chopped or ground walnuts and 1 teaspoon cinnamon. Add ¼ cup sweet wine or grape juice. Mix well, adding more liquid if it is very dry.

Estimated time: 10 minutes • Parve

This regal pillow is a cinch to make because there is no sewing involved. Personalize it by adding a "jeweled" monogram or other design to the center. It will have a prominent position — as well as be nice and comfortable — on your chair when you recline at the seder.

You can use the remaining polar fleece to make the afikomen bag on page 172.

no-sew pillow

What you will need:

- ☐ 1 yard polar fleece
- ☐ measuring tape or yard stick
- ☐ pencil
- ☐ pinking shears
- ☐ 4 safety pins or straight pins
- ☐ sharp scissors
- ☐ 12" square pillow form
- ☐ extra-strong wide and narrow double-sided red liner tape (we recommend Provo Craft Art Accentz Terrifically Tacky Tape)
- ☐ micro beads (we recommend Provo Craft Art Accentz Micro Beadz)

How to do it:

1. Use the measuring tape and pencil to measure and mark two 18" squares of polar fleece. Cut out the squares using pinking shears.

2. Place the squares, one on top of the other, on a flat surface and pin at each corner to keep them in place. Use a pencil to lightly measure and mark a 3" border around the square.

3. Cut 1"-wide strips, through both pieces of fleece, all around the pillow — stop cutting at the penciled line. When you get to each corner, snip off a 3"x3" square.

4. Keeping the fleece together, tie one front strip to the opposite back strip, in a double knot. Continue knotting all the strips on three sides.

5. Insert the pillow form into the opening. Knot the last side together.

6. Draw your initial or other design in pencil on the front of the pillow. Cut strips of double-sided tape to fit over the drawn outline; trim where necessary. Adhere tape to pillow over the outline.

7. Working with a small section of the letter at a time, pull the plastic covering from the tape and sprinkle micro beads to completely cover that section. Continue covering the letter with beads in this manner. Press down on beads to secure; shake any loose beads from the pillow.

Estimated time: 1 hour

Quick! Hide the afikomen!

At the seder, it's traditional for a piece of the middle matzo, called the afikomen, to be hidden by either the head of the seder or by the children participating. In either case, when the matzo is found or returned, the children receive (or are promised) a gift. This is all done in good spirits, to keep the children interested in the seder until the end, when the afikomen is eaten. Hide the afikomen in this beautiful bag that can be crafted to match your seder pillow — and let the fun begin!

afikomen bag

What you will need:

- ☐ ¼-yard polar fleece (we used the leftover fabric from the pillow on page 170)
- ☐ tape measure
- ☐ pencil
- ☐ pinking shears
- ☐ needle and thread
- ☐ sharp scissors
- ☐ 26" length of ½"-wide ribbon
- ☐ 2 tassels
- ☐ sequins or rhinestones, optional
- ☐ craft or fabric glue, optional

How to do it:

1. Measure and mark a 9"x22" rectangle on the back of the fleece. Cut out with pinking shears.

2. Fold the fleece in the middle, lengthwise, with the right side facing in. (If you are using fleece without a pattern, there is no right or wrong side; just make sure that the pencil marks are on the outside.) It should form a 9"x11" pouch.

3. With the needle and thread, or sewing machine, stitch the fleece together to form a pouch, leaving the top open.

4. Fold the top of the fleece pouch down so that there is a 1" cuff around the top.

5. Use your sharp scissors to cut ¼"-deep slits into the fold of the cuff, cutting through both layers at the same time. Cut 9 slits spaced 1" apart around the top of the pouch. Unfold the cuff.

6. Turn the pouch right-side-out. Thread the ribbon through the slits. Knot a tassel to each of the ribbon ends.

Optional: Decorate the front of the bag by gluing on rhinestones and/or sequins with craft glue or fabric glue.

Estimated time: 30 minutes – 45 minutes

On Pesach there is always a stack of matzot on the table during the holiday meals. This etched-glass matzo tray is a beautiful holder for the matzot everyone loves to eat.

Please note all the precautions listed on the bottle of etching cream before using it. Always wear gloves when you're handling the etching cream, wear an old shirt or apron, and work in a well-ventilated room. Be sure to store the etching cream away from small children.

matzo tray

What you will need:

- ☐ large round or square glass plate or charger
- ☐ contact paper or printer sticker paper, or die-cut sticker letters and design (we used the Provo Craft Cricut machine)
- ☐ permanent marker
- ☐ scissors
- ☐ disposable gloves
- ☐ etching cream, such as Armour Etch
- ☐ 1"-wide foam paintbrush
- ☐ paper towels

How to do it:

1. Photocopy the matzo word template and design (page 262) onto the printer sticker paper. Or, photocopy the template onto regular paper, cut out the letters and design, and trace the cut-outs with a permanent marker onto contact paper. Or, use die-cut sticker letters and design.

2. Carefully cut out the letters and design so that the edges are smooth, and arrange on the front of the plate. When you are satisfied with the layout, peel off the backing and rub the cut-out letters and design onto the plate so that they stick firmly. Smooth out any air bubbles with your fingers.

3. Put on the disposable gloves. Following the instructions on the bottle of etching cream, brush a thick coat of etching cream onto the entire front of the plate, covering the letters and design completely. Let set for five minutes.

4. Wearing the gloves, wash the plate under running water to remove the Armour Etch from the plate, and peel off all the stickers. Make sure there is no trace of etching cream left on the plate. Be sure to wear gloves when washing the paintbrush, as well, or discard brush without washing.

5. Dry the plate with paper towels.

Note: Hand-wash only.

Estimated time: 45 minutes

A trivet is especially useful on Pesach, when many counters and tables are covered with plastic coverings that could possibly become singed or ruined if a hot pot or dish is placed on them.

To make this trivet you'll need a ceramic tile; you may have one left over from a home-improvement project. One or two tiles can usually be obtained free, or for a nominal fee, from your local tile or home-improvement store.

trivet

What you will need:

- ☐ 8"-square ceramic tile
- ☐ enamel paint for ceramic and glass
- ☐ assorted narrow paintbrushes
- ☐ scissors
- ☐ thin cork to fit bottom of tile
- ☐ glue gun and glue sticks

How to do it:

1. Clean the tile with soap and water and dry very well. To prepare the tile for painting, follow the manufacturer's instructions that come with the paint you are using.

2. Paint on your design with the enamel paint. Allow to dry.

3. Cut a piece of cork to cover the back of the tile and glue it on with the glue gun.

Estimated time: 30 minutes
Drying time: as recommended by paint manufacturer

As a kid I always knew that Pesach was just around the corner when my mother would don her apron that read "Kosher for Pesach." (My brothers and I bought it for her one year and she loved it.) That meant that the house was already cleaned for the holiday and she was doing the really fun preparation — cooking the food.

Decorate an apron for that special cook or yourself so that you can protect his or her — or your — clothes while cooking.

"ready for pesach" apron

What you will need:

- ☐ matzo-patterned fabric (see resource page)
- ☐ iron-on fusible adhesive (17"x1 yard)
- ☐ iron
- ☐ scissors
- ☐ pencil
- ☐ white fabric apron
- ☐ iron-on letters or dimensional fabric paint in assorted colors
- ☐ piece of stiff cardboard
- ☐ brown dimensional fabric paint

How to do it:

1. Iron a large piece of iron-on fusible adhesive to the back of the patterned fabric, following the manufacturer's instructions. Use scissors to cut the adhesive-backed fabric into the matzo shape(s) of your choice.

2. With a pencil, lightly outline where the letters and pictures should be on the apron front. With a hot iron, press the matzo shape(s) onto the center of the apron, following manufacturer's directions. If you are using iron-on lettering, press these on as well. If you are using dimensional fabric paint for the lettering, place the apron front-side-up onto a piece of cardboard. Paint the letters with dimensional fabric paints over the outlined letters. Allow to dry.

3. Place the apron front-side-up onto a piece of cardboard. Outline the matzo shape with the brown dimensional fabric paint. Allow to dry.

Estimated time: 30 minutes
Drying time: as recommended by paint manufacturer

The plagues with which the Egyptians were punished because they would not allow the Jews to leave Egypt are called the makot. This fun matching game will help children remember the names of the plagues as well as what happened to the Egyptians during that time.

This game is quick and easy to make as well as to play. Laminating the cards will make them more durable; this can be done at a local copy shop.

makot matching game

What you will need:

- ☐ 3 (8½"x11") sheets white cardstock or thick paper
- ☐ 3 (12"x12") sheets colored cardstock or scrapbook paper
- ☐ scissors
- ☐ markers
- ☐ glue stick

How to do it:

1. Fold one sheet of white paper in half. Then fold the paper in half and then in half again. Unfold the paper. The folds will have divided the paper into 8 equal rectangles.

2. Repeat step one with the other two papers. Cut out the rectangles; you will only need 20, so there will be four extra.

3. Draw a picture of a different makah on ten of the rectangles or download a clip art picture from your computer and glue to rectangles.

4. Write or print the Hebrew and English names of each makah on the other ten rectangles.

5. Fold the 12"x12" papers in the same manner that you did the white paper. Cut out the colored rectangles.

6. Center each white rectangle on each colored rectangle and glue into place, centering the white rectangles so that a colored border is visible.

Optional: Have the cards laminated at a copy shop or office center. Punch a hole in the top right corner of each card and place on a metal ring for storage.

Note: The makot cards pictured here were made using color copies of illustrations in the ArtScroll Children's Haggadah; used with permission.

Estimated time: 45 minutes

CHOL HAMOED PESACH PICNIC

The intermediate days of the holiday, known as Chol Hamoed, often give families time to spend together, but if your family is comprised of children of varying ages, half the time is usually spent figuring out where to go — amusement park or zoo, museum or batting range — no one can seem to agree. Here's a great way to spend some time with your family on Chol Hamoed in a way that everyone can enjoy. Spend some time outdoors enjoying the wonderful start of spring. Go on a hike or bike ride through a wooded trail or play at the beach, which is usually deserted at this time of year. After expending all that energy, follow up with a yummy Pesach picnic.

■ Set up:

The great thing about a picnic is that there is no real set-up involved. You do, however, need to pack the food and utensils so that they are easy to take to your picnic site. You may wish to use backpacks to share the transporting chore among family members. Pack salads and cut-up fruits and vegetables separately. Place all perishables in an insulated backpack or use ice packs around each container. Don't forget non-perishables, such as matzo, brownies, macaroons, chocolate, apples, oranges, and/or bananas. Another backpack should hold disposable plates, plastic silverware, napkins, and paper towels. One final backpack will be needed to hold all the extras, such as a blanket, hand sanitizer, wipes, bug spray, and a garbage bag for taking the trash back with you — don't forget to leave the area as clean as (or cleaner than) you found it.

■ Food:

All that activity will leave you hungry — so take along filling food. We pack a basic lunch when we picnic. Tuna salad, deviled eggs (page 186), vegetable cream cheese, and guacamole placed in containers are all easy tote-along options; and they all taste delicious when spread on matzo.

Cut up carrot sticks, celery spears, olives, and cherry tomatoes are great accompaniments. Macaroons (page 188), Pesach brownies (page 189), fresh fruit, and chocolate are the perfect picnic desserts.

Pack serving-size amounts of mixed nuts and dried fruits in ziplock snack bags for an energizing snack or mid-hike munch.

········· chicken kabobs ·········

What you will need:

- ☐ 18-20 skewers
- ☐ shallow rectangular container
- ☐ sharp knife and cutting board
- ☐ large plastic ziplock food storage bag
- ☐ glass mixing bowl
- ☐ measuring cup and spoons
- ☐ fork or whisk
- ☐ grill pan

Ingredients:

- ☐ 1 package chicken cutlets (approx. 8 cutlets)
- ☐ ¼ cup lemon juice
- ☐ 3 tablespoons olive oil
- ☐ 3 cubes frozen crushed garlic (or 3 cloves fresh garlic, minced)
- ☐ 1-2 tablespoon fresh basil, chopped, or 1 teaspoon dried basil
- ☐ ½ teaspoon kosher salt
- ☐ ¼ teaspoon pepper
- ☐ zucchini, cut into chunks; red and yellow peppers, cut into chunks; cherry or grape tomatoes, optional

Chicken kabobs are quick to prepare for a Chol Hamoed dinner. The chicken is placed in a marinade, resulting in a great flavor. While it marinates, you can cut up a salad and set the table — you'll have dinner done in a jiffy.

How to do it:

1. Place bamboo skewers into the shallow container filled halfway with cold water. Soak skewers for 15 minutes.

2. While the skewers are soaking, cut all visible fat from chicken, and cut chicken cutlets into 1"-wide strips. Place the chicken strips into a plastic ziplock bag.

3. To make marinade, pour all the remaining ingredients into the glass bowl and mix with a fork or whisk. Carefully pour the marinade into bag. Press the air out of the bag and seal the bag. Place the bag with the chicken in the fridge for 15–30 minutes.

4. Remove chicken strips from the marinade and thread one or two strips onto each skewer. You can thread the vegetables onto the skewers as well, alternating with chicken or on separate skewers.

5. Place the grill pan over medium-high heat, or heat up a barbeque grill.

6. Grill the kabobs for 3 minutes on each side, or until browned on the outside and center is no longer pink. Serve immediately.

Estimated prep time: 20 minutes
Marinating time: 15 – 30 minutes
Cook time: 6 minutes
Meat • Yield: 18-20 kabobs

········ deviled eggs ········

What you will need:

- ☐ medium pot
- ☐ small bowl
- ☐ measuring spoons
- ☐ knife

Ingredients:

- ☐ 6 boiled eggs
- ☐ ¼ cup mayonnaise
- ☐ salt and pepper to taste
- ☐ garnishing options: paprika, snipped chives, and/or thyme

The ubiquitous egg is ever-prevalent in a host of Pesach recipes. Any "balabusta" worth her salt uses dozens of them throughout the holiday, beating and whipping them to a froth in place of flour and leavening agents. Here we give the humble egg its chance to star on its own as a delicious snack or appetizer.

How to do it:

1. Peel the eggs and cut in half lengthwise. Scoop out the yolks and place into the small bowl. Place the whites on a plate or tray and set aside.

2. Add the mayonnaise, salt, and pepper to the egg yolks. Mash well with a fork until the ingredients are combined and smooth.

3. Divide the mixture evenly and place a mound into each egg-white half. Garnish with paprika, snipped chives, and/or thyme, according to taste.

Estimated prep time: 10 minutes
Parve • Yield: 6 servings

How to Boil Eggs:

Place eggs in a pot large enough so they are not crowded. Add cold water to completely cover eggs. Place pot over medium-high heat and bring to a boil. Remove the pot from heat and cover. Let stand, covered for 12-15 minutes. Rinse the eggs in the pot under cold running water and remove from the pot.

Cook time: 20 minutes

········ walnut macaroons ········

What you will need:

- ☐ cookie sheets
- ☐ parchment paper
- ☐ small bowl
- ☐ electric mixer
- ☐ measuring cups
- ☐ spatula
- ☐ ziplock bag
- ☐ scissors

Ingredients:

- ☐ 4 eggs
- ☐ 2 cups sugar
- ☐ ½ cup ground walnuts

When I was a kid, I loved baking Pesach cakes and cookies. Beating the egg whites with sugar until they were stiff was my favorite part of the baking process. I would bake dozens of these egg-white-based cookies and hide them away in the back of cabinets so that my brothers wouldn't eat them before the holiday. (Why eat a macaroon before Pesach if you can eat a regular cookie? That was my thought; they thought otherwise.)

One of my brothers is convinced that there still is a container filled with cookies that no one has ever found, still hidden away in the basement closet of my parents' old home.

How to do it:

1. Preheat oven to 350°F. Cover cookie sheets with parchment paper. Set aside.

2. Crack open one egg at a time and carefully separate the egg white from the yolk. Place the yolks into a small bowl and reserve for another purpose.

3. Place the egg whites into the mixer bowl and beat on high until very foamy.

4. Slowly add the sugar. Beat on high until the egg whites are stiff and shiny.

5. Use a spatula to gently fold in the ground walnuts.

6. Use the spatula to spoon the mixture into the ziplock bag. Seal the bag and snip the tip off one corner.

7. Squeeze out small mounds of macaroon mixture onto the cookie sheet. Place mounds ½-inch apart.

8. Bake in the oven for 15 minutes. Allow to cool for ½-hour in the oven after turning off the heat. Remove from oven and allow to cool completely.

Estimated prep time: 15 minutes
Bake time: 15 minutes
Cooling time: 30 minutes in turned-off oven
Parve • Yield: 3 dozen macaroons

easy brownies

What you will need:

- [ ] parchment paper
- [ ] 9"x13" baking pan
- [ ] electric mixer
- [ ] measuring cup and spoons
- [ ] liquid measuring cup
- [ ] spatula
- [ ] wire rack

Ingredients:

- [ ] 4 eggs
- [ ] 1½ cups sugar
- [ ] 1 cup oil
- [ ] ½ cup cocoa
- [ ] ¾ cup potato starch
- [ ] ½ cup chopped nuts

My sister makes the absolute best brownies for Pesach. Yum!

How to do it:

1. Preheat the oven to 350°F. Cut a piece of parchment paper to fit the bottom and up the sides of the baking pan. Set aside.

2. Crack eggs and place into the mixer bowl. Beat on high speed until eggs are light and foamy. Add sugar and oil and beat until well combined.

3. Lower the mixer speed and add the cocoa and potato starch. Mix just until combined (don't overmix).

4. Use your spatula to gently fold the nuts into the batter.

5. Pour the mixture into the prepared pan. Place into hot oven and bake for 45 minutes.

6. Remove from the oven and place pan on a wire rack to cool. Cut into 1½" squares while warm.

Estimated prep time: 15 minutes

Bake time: 45 minutes

Parve • Yield: 24 servings

strawberry sorbet

What you will need:

- [ ] food processor
- [ ] dry and liquid measuring cups
- [ ] large freezer-safe food container
- [ ] spatula

Ingredients:

- [ ] 2 (14-ounce) bags frozen strawberries
- [ ] ½ cup sugar
- [ ] ¼ cup lemon juice
- [ ] ¼ cup dark grape juice

How to do it:

1. Place slightly defrosted strawberries into a food processor bowl fitted with the S-blade. Process on high until strawberries are completely puréed.

2. Add the sugar and juices. Process 1 minute, until combined.

3. Pour the sorbet mixture into the container and smooth the top with a spatula. Place into the freezer.

4. After about 2 hours, remove container from the freezer. Place the partially frozen sorbet into the food processor bowl and process again until whipped. Return sorbet to freezer container and freeze until needed.

Estimated prep time: 15 minutes, divided

Freeze time: 4 hours, divided

Parve • Yield: 8 servings

SHAVUOT

It was on a mountain in the desert — neither the highest mountain, nor the most beautiful mountain, but apparently the holiest — that the Jewish People received their greatest gift. It was at Mount Sinai that the Jews were given the Torah and thus became the Jewish nation. This momentous event is commemorated on the joyful holiday of Shavuot with the sounds of Torah study emanating from synagogues and Jewish study halls late on Shavuot night and the reading of the Ten Commandments on Shavuot day.

In one of the loveliest traditions of this spring holiday, our synagogues and homes are decorated with flowers to celebrate the fact that Mount Sinai, an otherwise barren desert mountain, bloomed on the day that the Torah was given.

In addition to decorating your home with garlands of fresh flowers and shiny green leaves, you can create a lasting floral display with silk flowers or craft sticks. They'll grace your home long after the cheesecake — another delicious Shavuot tradition — has disappeared.

A topiary is a bush or tree that is sculpted, cut, and/or trained to grow into a specific shape. This arrangement mimics the art of true topiaries by forming a silk flower bush into a rounded shape.

flower topiary

What you will need:

- ☐ flower pot
- ☐ scissors
- ☐ piece of Styrofoam to fit into the flower pot
- ☐ silk flower bush of your choice
- ☐ 2 twist ties
- ☐ green/brown ribbon or floral tape
- ☐ glue gun and glue sticks
- ☐ craft glue
- ☐ Spanish moss
- ☐ decorative ribbon

How to do it:

1. Place the piece of Styrofoam into the flower pot. Trim the Styrofoam if necessary (it should not stick out of the pot). Set aside.

2. Take the flower bush and grasp all the branches, holding them tightly together. Fasten a twist tie tightly around the branches directly under the flowers. If necessary, fasten the other twist tie around the middle of the stems to keep them together. This will form the topiary's stem.

3. Bend the stems until the flowers form a rounded shape.

4. Use the glue gun and glue sticks to attach the ribbon or floral tape to the top of the stem, just under the flowers. Wind the ribbon around the stem, completely covering the twist ties. Hot glue the ribbon to the bottom of the stem and trim the excess ribbon, if necessary.

5. Poke the stem through the center of the Styrofoam in the flower pot. Push down on the stem so that it reaches deep into the pot. Glue it into place if it feels wobbly.

6. Spread the craft glue over the Styrofoam and place clumps of Spanish moss on the wet glue to completely cover the Styrofoam.

7. Tie a ribbon into a bow around the center of the stem.

Estimated time: 20 minutes

Even a very young child can craft beautiful flowers for Shavuot. My five-year-old son, Gad Shua, easily made the samples for this book.

craft stick flowers

What you will need:

- ☐ 4-6 colored regular or jumbo craft sticks per flower
- ☐ white glue
- ☐ colored flat buttons
- ☐ scissors
- ☐ tall drinking glass or vase
- ☐ jelly beans, marbles, or gravel, optional

How to do it:

1. Lay one craft stick on a table or flat surface. Put a dab of glue on the center of the stick.

2. Place another stick across it so that the two sticks form a wide "X."

3. Put a dab of glue on the center of the top stick and place another stick across the middle of the "X."

4. Continue gluing on 1–3 more sticks so that the joined sticks look like a full flower.

5. Put a dab of glue on the center of the top stick and place a button on it. Let the flower dry.

6. Make additional flowers by repeating steps 1–5.

7. Glue a green craft stick onto the back of the dry flower. This will be the flower's stem. Cut another green stick in half to form leaves. Glue one or two leaves to the back of the stem. Let dry. Repeat for remaining flowers.

8. Display the flowers in a tall drinking glass or vase.

Optional: Fill the glass or vase with colored jelly beans, marbles, or gravel. Push the flower stems into the filler.

Estimated time: 15 – 30 minutes
Drying time: 30 minutes – 1 hour

Decorating cupcakes or muffins as mini Har Sinais is a fun way to get young children involved in the Shavuot holiday.

mini har sinai

What you will need:

- [ ] spatula or spoon
- [ ] 1 (12-ounce) container vanilla frosting
- [ ] medium bowl
- [ ] liquid or gel green food coloring
- [ ] 1 dozen unfrosted cupcakes or 6 muffins
- [ ] offset spatula
- [ ] flower-shaped sprinkles
- [ ] vanilla wafers, optional

How to do it:

1. Use the spatula or spoon to transfer the frosting to the bowl. Place 2-3 drops of food coloring into the frosting.

2. Mix the food coloring into the frosting with your spatula or spoon. If the color is too light, add in more food coloring, one drop at a time. Mix well before adding additional food coloring to avoid streaks. Note that the color may deepen after standing.

3. Working with one cupcake or muffin at a time, use an offset spatula to spread icing all over the top of the cupcake or muffin.

4. Sprinkle flower-shaped sprinkles on top of the frosting.

Optional: Place two vanilla wafers on top to resemble luchot.

Estimated time: 30 minutes
Dairy or Parve • Yield: 1 dozen cupcakes or 6 muffins

Who says flowers belong only in gardens and vases? These flower accessories show you that flowers are perfect just about anywhere.

flower hair accessories

What you will need:

- ☐ ribbon scraps
- ☐ glue gun and glue sticks
- ☐ French clip barrette and/ or ponytail holder
- ☐ silk flowers of your choice
- ☐ scissors

How to do it:

Flower Barrette:

1. Use the glue gun and glue sticks to glue a piece of ribbon to the top of the barrette, tucking the ends under and gluing them down.

2. Separate the flowers from the stem. Use your scissors to trim off as much of the underside of the flower as you can.

3. Hot glue one or more flowers to the barrette. Press down on the flower(s) to secure. Allow to dry.

Flower Pony Holder:

1. Separate one large flat flower (such as a sunflower or peony) from its stem. With scissors, trim any remaining stem from the back of the flower.

2. Use the glue gun and glue sticks to glue the back of the flower to the ponytail holder.

3. Cut a small piece of ribbon and hot glue it over the back of the flower where it is attached to the ponytail holder. Part of the ponytail holder should be sandwiched between the flower and the ribbon. The ribbon should not be visible from the flower side of the ponytail holder. Press down to secure the ribbon to the flower. Allow to dry.

Estimated time: 5 – 10 minutes

These beautiful napkin rings and napkins will dress up your holiday table.

beaded napkin rings

What you will need:

- ☐ ruler
- ☐ metal wire, 22-gauge
- ☐ strong scissors or wire cutters
- ☐ flat-nose pliers
- ☐ approx. 15 large glass or plastic beads per ring
- ☐ approx. 10–15 spacer beads or rondells per ring
- ☐ beading elastic, optional

How to do it:

1. For each ring: With the ruler, measure an 8" length of wire and cut with scissors or wire cutters. Use pliers to form a tight wire loop at one end.

2. String a spacer bead onto open end of wire and then add a large bead. Continue stringing beads until 1" of wire remains, ending with a spacer bead.

3. Thread the 1" of wire into the loop. With pliers, twist the wire around to close the napkin ring securely.

Optional: Use beading elastic instead of the wire. String the beads on in the same manner and knot to close.

Estimated time: 10 minutes per ring

stamped napkins

What you will need:

- ☐ self-adhesive felt
- ☐ fine-point permanent marker
- ☐ scissors
- ☐ wooden blocks and/or empty film canisters
- ☐ acrylic paint
- ☐ disposable plastic plate
- ☐ small flat paintbrush
- ☐ paper towels
- ☐ cotton or linen napkins
- ☐ cardboard
- ☐ iron

How to do it:

1. Photocopy and cut out leaf- and flower-shaped templates (page 255). Use the marker to trace templates onto backing of felt. With scissors, cut out shapes.

2. Peel off felt backing and adhere shapes to blocks or film canisters.

3. Pour some paint onto the plate. Press the felt flower into the paint or brush on paint. With a paper towel, wipe off excess paint.

4. Place a napkin on the cardboard. Stamp shapes firmly on the napkin. Lift stamp carefully so as not to smudge the flowers.

5. Continue stamping, dipping stamps into paint before each use.

6. Dry thoroughly. To set colors, press with hot iron before use or washing.

Estimated time: 45 minutes

Drying time: 2 – 4 hours

SHAVUOT DAIRY DESSERT DISPLAY

I love Shavuot morning; everyone gets up late after a long night spent learning Torah in shul. We usually eat a dairy Yom Tov meal in the early afternoon and then invite several neighbors for dessert.

Since flowers are a dominant theme of Shavuot, decorating the table will be a cinch — just put out all your flower bouquets and use extra vases and flowerpots as serving pieces and catch-alls. For added drama, before Yom Tov, craft some huge tissue-paper flowers and place them into a tall vase in the center of the table — you can also make some small ones to decorate the chairs.

■ Set up:

All the cakes and pies on this dessert menu are baked in advance. Just pop them out of the fridge and freezer and set them out on platters and cake plates; everyone will be thrilled with the effort you've put into setting it up.

Before the meal, set a separate dessert table in the dining room or in a room adjacent to the dining room. Lay the tablecloth and set out the platters and cake plates. Add cups and napkins, placing dessert forks and spoons into small flower vases or flower pots. Intersperse small flower bouquets between the serving dishes.

■ Food:

Serve your favorite cheesecakes (pages 208-209) and dairy cakes. Mini cheese Danishes, Har Sinai cupcakes (page 196), and other pastries are yummy as well. Serve fruit skewers with dipping sauce (page 206) and layered ice pops (facing page) — they're a great frozen treat.

For drinks, nothing beats iced tea, iced coffee, lemonade (we love pink lemonade), or cold chocolate milk on a hot day.

········ layered ice pops ·········

What you will need:

- [ ] sharp knife and cutting board
- [ ] liquid measuring cup
- [ ] blender
- [ ] spoon
- [ ] 6-8 ice pop molds or 5-ounce cups with craft sticks

Ingredients:

For each layer

- [ ] 1 cup juice: apple, orange, grape, pineapple, or mango
- [ ] 1 cup fruit, fresh, frozen or canned, including mangoes, strawberries, kiwis, blueberries, pineapples, apricots, or peaches

These refreshing treats (see page 202) look and taste delicious and are lots of fun to make. Experiment with fruit and juice combinations to come up with your favorite. If you are using frozen fruit, let it defrost slightly before placing it into the blender.

How to do it:

1. Wash, peel, and cut the fruit into chunks with a sharp knife if necessary. (If you are using canned or frozen fruit you can skip this step.)

2. Measure one cup juice and place into the blender. Measure one cup prepared fruit and place into blender.

3. Cover blender and blend on high until smooth.

4. Spoon mixture into the ice pop molds, dividing the mixture evenly among the molds. Each mold should be half-full.

5. Freeze for 1–1½ hours.

6. Repeat steps 1–3, using a clean blender container and a different combination of juice and fruit. Take ice pops out of the freezer and spoon this mixture over the first layer, filling the mold or cup to the top. Place the ice pop handle or a craft stick into the mixture.

7. Freeze until solid, about 2–3 hours.

8. To serve, run warm tap water on the outside of the mold to release the ice pop from the mold.

Optional: For single-flavor pops, double the fruit and juice combination and follow steps 1–3. Divide evenly among molds, insert handles, and freeze for 2–3 hours.

Estimated prep time: 15 minutes
Total freeze time: 4–5 hours
Parve • Yield: 6-8 ice pops

········ fruit skewers with dipping sauce ·········

What you will need:

- ☐ sharp knife and cutting board
- ☐ skewers, as needed
- ☐ small bowl
- ☐ tablespoon
- ☐ large serving tray
- ☐ microplane grater or zester, optional

Fruit Skewer Ingredients:

- ☐ 1 pint strawberries
- ☐ ½ pineapple
- ☐ 2 kiwis
- ☐ 2 star fruits

Honey-Yogurt Sauce Ingredients:

- ☐ 1 (8-ounce) container vanilla yogurt
- ☐ 2 tablespoons honey
- ☐ 1 tablespoon orange juice
- ☐ 1 orange, optional

These fruit skewers are a treat to look at as well as to eat. You can substitute your favorite fruits for the ones shown here. The sauce is also delicious spooned over a cup of cut-up fruit with granola sprinkled on top.

How to do it:

1. Wash the strawberries and star fruit well. With a sharp knife, remove the green tops from the strawberries. If the berries are large, cut in half vertically.

2. Cut the peel from the ½ pineapple and cut the pineapple vertically down the center, into two wedges. Remove the hard core from the inner edge of each pineapple wedge. Slice the pineapple into ½"-thick wedges.

3. Peel the kiwis and slice into ¼"-thick slices.

4. Slice the star fruit into ¼"-thick slices.

5. Thread slices of star fruit, kiwi, pineapple, and a strawberry or strawberry half onto each skewer.

6. Prepare the honey-yogurt dipping sauce: Pour the yogurt into the small bowl and add the honey and orange juice. Mix well so that the honey is incorporated.

7. Place the bowl of sauce on the tray. Arrange the fruit skewers on the tray around the bowl of sauce.

Optional: For a more pronounced citrus flavor, add orange zest to the sauce: Wash an orange well and dry. Grate the orange peel with a microplane grater or zester. Take care not to grate the white pith. Grate 1 teaspoon of zest and mix into the sauce.

Estimated prep time: 30 minutes
Dairy • Yield: will vary according to amount of fruit used

mini cheesecakes

What you will need:

- [ ] 3 (6-cup) muffin tins
- [ ] cupcake holders
- [ ] stand mixer or hand mixer with large bowl
- [ ] measuring cups
- [ ] teaspoon
- [ ] spatula or tablespoon

Ingredients:

- [ ] 18 Swiss Fudge cookies
- [ ] 2 (8-ounce) containers cream cheese, softened
- [ ] ½ cup sugar
- [ ] 1 teaspoon vanilla extract
- [ ] 2 eggs

There's a surprise layer of chocolate at the bottom of these scrumptious little cheesecake delights.

How to do it:

1. Preheat oven to 325°F. Place one cupcake holder into each cup of the muffin tins.
2. Place a Swiss Fudge cookie into each cupcake holder. Set aside.
3. Place the cream cheese into the mixer bowl and beat on medium speed. Add the sugar and vanilla and increase the speed to high. Beat well until the mixture is fluffy.
4. Lower the mixer speed and add the eggs. Beat until combined.
5. Use your spatula or tablespoon to fill the prepared muffin tins with cheesecake batter. Fill each cupcake holder till the top.
6. Place the muffin tins into the hot oven and bake for 25 minutes.
7. After 25 minutes, turn off the oven but leave the cheesecakes in the oven with the door slightly ajar for another 15 minutes before removing them.
8. Cool on a wire rack.

Estimated prep time: 15 minutes
Bake time: 25 minutes
Dairy • Yield: 18 servings

········· frozen cheesecake ·········

This no-bake cheesecake (see photo on page 202) is my family's favorite Shavuot dessert because it tastes like ice cream and cheesecake mixed together. Who could think of a better combination?

You can bake the crust yourself or save time by using a purchased graham-cracker pie crust and skip steps 1 – 6.

What you will need:

Pie Crust:

- ☐ food processor or rolling pin and ziplock bag
- ☐ large mixing bowl
- ☐ spoon
- ☐ 8"-9" pie pan or tart pan
- ☐ electric mixer
- ☐ measuring cup and spoons
- ☐ spatula
- ☐ aluminum foil
- ☐ knife

Ingredients:

- ☐ 9 double graham crackers and ⅓ cup butter, softened, or 1 purchased graham-cracker pie crust
- ☐ 8 ounces whipped cream cheese
- ☐ ½ cup farmer's cheese
- ☐ ½ cup vanilla yogurt
- ☐ ½ cup sugar
- ☐ 1 teaspoon vanilla sugar
- ☐ 1 pint strawberries or fruit and berries of your choice

How to do it:

1. Preheat the oven to 350°F.

2. Place the graham crackers in the food processor and blend on high until finely ground. Or, place graham crackers into a heavy-duty ziplock bag and crush with a rolling pin.

3. Place the graham cracker crumbs into the large bowl. Add the softened butter.

4. Mix the butter and graham cracker crumbs with a spoon (or rub together with your fingers) until combined.

5. Press the graham cracker mixture into the bottom and up the side of the pie pan or tart pan.

6. Bake for 10 minutes. Remove the pie shell from the oven and let cool.

7. Place whipped cream cheese, farmer's cheese, yogurt, sugar, and vanilla sugar into the mixer bowl. Beat at low speed until all ingredients are combined. Increase speed to high and beat until the mixture is smooth and fluffy.

8. Pour the mixture into the prepared or purchased pie crust and smooth with the spatula.

9. Cover with aluminum foil and freeze until firm.

10. Remove the pie from the freezer and thaw for one hour before serving.

11. Wash the strawberries well and cut off the green tops.

12. Slice the strawberries and arrange the slices around the top of the cheesecake. You can use other fruits or berries of your choice.

Estimated prep time: 1 hour plus freeze time
Baking time: 10 minutes
Dairy • Yield: 8 servings

SHABBAT

Wonderful, wonderful Shabbat! It's an oasis of pleasure and serenity, an island of quiet in a noisy sea. All week long we're running and bustling about. Work, school, play, everything is done at a frenetic pace, but when Shabbat comes that all stops. Because whether you call Saturday — Shabbat, Shabbos, or Sabbath, it means the same thing — rest. For on Shabbat the Jewish people cease all work and spend the day resting and reconnecting with family.

The meals on Shabbat are especially good-quality family time with everyone enjoying hearty food, melodious singing, and precious words of Torah. While every Shabbat table is beautiful, it is still that much lovelier when we put our creative talents to work to enhance it. It is exciting to braid and bake our own homemade challah and cover it with a decorated challah cover. Or you can choose to craft Shabbat candlesticks to hold the candles that are lit to usher in the Shabbat or to embellish the Shabbat song books with suede covers and golden tassels.

While it is hard to say goodbye to Shabbat as the day ends, the transition will be eased by utilizing a havdalah candle that's our very own creation, reminding us that the special Shabbat atmosphere — and the gorgeous Shabbat table crafts — will be back in just one week!

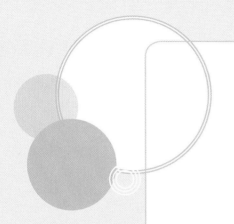

One of the special mitzvot that Jewish women fulfill is to light candles to usher in the Shabbat. This mitzvah is performed each week on Friday before sundown.

The candlesticks that hold the Shabbat candles come in a myriad of shapes, materials, and designs. We have designed these beaded candlesticks using small bud vases from a major discount store, but they can be made with traditional glass or metal candlesticks or rounded glass candleholders. Crafting candlesticks for yourself or a loved one to use on Shabbat will make the candlelighting experience even more meaningful.

shabbat candlesticks

What you will need:

- [ ] 2 small bud vases, glass candleholders, or candlesticks
- [ ] measuring tape and pencil
- [ ] scissors
- [ ] extra-strong wide or narrow double-sided red liner tape (we recommend Provo Craft Art Accentz Terrifically Tacky Tape)
- [ ] paper plate
- [ ] micro beads in assorted colors
- [ ] small glass beads or stones in assorted colors, optional

How to do it:

1. Decide how much of the candlestick you wish to cover with beads. Design the pattern you want, using the micro beads and the small beads. Measure and cut the adhesive tape to the size and shape that you need.

2. Press the adhesive tape onto the candlestick. Trim the ends if necessary. Press down firmly to ensure that it is attached securely. If you are doing a pattern in a variety of colored beads, attach only one strip of tape at a time so that the beads don't accidentally stick to the wrong spot.

3. Place the candlestick on the paper plate. Working with one section or strip at a time, peel the backing off the adhesive tape and gently attach the micro beads and the small glass beads or stones, if using, to that section. Make sure that all the beads are firmly attached and that there are no empty spaces before you begin another section.

4. Replace extra beads in their container.

Note: To prevent delicate glass candlesticks from cracking as candles burn down, use metal or disposable candleholders.

Estimated time: 30 minutes – 45 minutes

This handcrafted challah cover will make a beautiful addition to your Shabbat table. Since you decorate it as you wish with dimensional fabric paint, this project can be as simple or as elaborate as you choose to make it. Bear in mind that there is considerable drying time involved.

challah cover

What you will need:

- ☐ ½ yard velvet fabric
- ☐ tape measure or yardstick
- ☐ pencil or chalk
- ☐ scissors
- ☐ dimensional fabric paint in assorted colors
- ☐ thin paintbrushes, optional
- ☐ disposable plastic plate
- ☐ 2 yards trim or fringe
- ☐ fabric glue
- ☐ 4 straight pins

How to do it:

1. Use a tape measure to measure a 14½"x17" rectangle of the velvet fabric. Mark the measurements with the pencil or chalk on the back of the velvet; then cut out with scissors.

2. Using a pencil, outline the letters and design of your choice onto the front of the velvet. Go over the outlines using dimensional fabric paint tubes. Or, squeeze small amounts of dimensional fabric paint onto a plastic plate; use the paint and paintbrushes to brush on the design. You may need more than one coat of paint, because the velvet absorbs it. Let dry as recommended by the paint manufacturer, about 24 hours.

3. Spread a line of fabric glue around the edge of the challah cover. Starting at one corner, glue the trim down along the edge. At the next corner fold trim under to form a right angle (there will be a 45°-angled section to glue under), glue folded section to corner, and secure with a straight pin to hold the fold in place. Continue attaching trim in this manner until the edge is completely covered with trim.

4. Use scissors to cut off excess trim, if any. Let dry as recommended by the glue manufacturer, about 24 hours.

5. Remove straight pins.

Estimated time: 45 minutes

Total drying time: as recommended by the paint and glue manufacturers, about 48 hours, divided

No Shabbat table is complete without bentchers. "Bentch" is the Yiddish word for "bless," referring to the Bircat Hamazon — Grace After Meals — that is said after eating a meal at which bread was eaten. These small books contain the Bircat Hamazon and, often, also the lyrics of the songs frequently sung at the Shabbat meals. Guests at weddings or other Jewish celebrations often receive bentchers as keepsakes.

We have quite a collection of bentchers that we've received at numerous events. In order to give the assorted bentchers a uniform look, I covered them in suede paper and added matching tassels. They are now a beautiful addition to our Shabbat table.

decorated bentchers

What you will need:

- [ ] bentchers, as many as desired, all the same size
- [ ] suede or velour self-adhesive paper, 1 sheet per bentcher; or suede adhesive-backed drawer liner
- [ ] ruler
- [ ] pencil
- [ ] scissors or paper cutter
- [ ] X-Acto knife
- [ ] cording
- [ ] tassels, 1 per bentcher

How to do it:

1. Open one bentcher to the center and lay it flat, face down, on your work surface. Measure the length and width of the bentcher with your ruler. Mark those measurements on the back of the suede paper and cut the suede paper with scissors or a paper cutter. (Alternatively, you can open up the bentcher and lay it flat on the back of the suede paper, trace around the bentcher with a pencil, and then cut out.)

2. Remove the paper backing from the suede paper and adhere to the bentcher cover. Make sure that it is attached smoothly and securely. Open the bentcher and check to see if the edges are neat and that the suede paper is flush with the bentcher cover. If necessary, use an X-Acto knife to trim any excess suede paper to assure a neat look.

3. Cut a length of cording to fit around the spine of the bentcher, plus an inch or two to form the knot. Knot the two ends together and slip around the center fold of the opened bentcher. Trim any excess cording. Knot the tassel to the top of the cording.

Estimated time: 30 minutes for each bentcher

It's always fun to have guests sleep over in your home; moreover, hosting Shabbat guests is a wonderful way to fulfill the mitzvah of Hachnassat Orchim — hospitality. Whoever your guests are, they will certainly appreciate a welcoming, quiet room in which to rest. Placing this hanging sign on the doorknob of your guest room does the trick of welcoming your guests, and when it's time to rest they can turn it over and let everyone know not to disturb them.

guest doorknob hanger

What you will need:

- ☐ wooden or chipboard doorknob hanger
- ☐ pencil
- ☐ 1-2 (12"x12") sheets scrapbook paper
- ☐ brown ink pad
- ☐ scissors
- ☐ craft glue and/or tape runner
- ☐ large chipboard letters or stickers reading "welcome," "hi," and "shh"; or use alphabet stickers
- ☐ embellishments: ribbon scraps, rickrack, flat fabric flowers, buttons, glitter

How to do it:

1. Place the doorknob hanger on the back of the scrapbook paper. With a pencil, trace around the doorknob hanger and the center circle. Trace it again onto the back of a second piece of paper or on the same sheet of paper.

2. Cut out the two outlined shapes with scissors. For the center hole, poke the middle of the circle carefully with the scissors, and cut through the circle. Carefully cut out the traced outline of the circle.

3. Glue or tape one shape to each side of the doorknob hanger.

4. Pat the ink pad gently along the edges of the scrapbook paper to give it an antiqued look.

5. Glue the letters spelling your welcoming message onto one side of the hanger.

6. Glue chipboard letters to spell "Shh!" onto the other side of the hanger.

7. Cut one ribbon and two pieces of rickrack the length needed to wrap around both sides of the hanger. Glue the ribbon around the bottom third of the hanger, overlapping slightly on the front. Glue the first piece of rickrack ½" below the ribbon. Glue the second rickrack ½" under the first.

8. Use a piece of ribbon to form a bow; glue it over the overlapped ribbon, near the side of the hanger (see photo). Glue a flower on top of the bow. Glue a button to the center of the flower.

9. Repeat step 8 on the back of the hanger. Embellish as desired.

Estimated time: 30 minutes – 45 minutes

Prepare a basket full of necessities that you think your guests might need or want during their stay — it will make them feel especially welcome!

feel-at-home basket

What you will need:

- ☐ ruler and pencil
- ☐ cardstock
- ☐ scissors
- ☐ corner punch
- ☐ hole puncher
- ☐ 2 reinforcements or 1 eyelet and eyelet setter
- ☐ markers or alphabet stamps and stamp pad
- ☐ assorted ribbon scraps
- ☐ large basket or bin
- ☐ stapler
- ☐ fabric flower
- ☐ craft glue and/or glue dots

How to do it:

1. Use your ruler and pencil to measure and outline a 3"x5" rectangle on a piece of cardstock. Use the scissors to cut out the rectangle.

2. Use the corner punch to round two short edges of the rectangle to form the top of the tag. With the hole puncher, punch a hole in the middle of the rounded corners toward the top of the tag.

3. Reinforce the hole by placing reinforcement stickers around the hole on both sides of the tag. Or, use an eyelet setter to place an eyelet around the hole, following manufacturer's instructions.

4. Print "Feel at Home" with markers or stamps on the center of the tag.

5. Cut ribbon scraps into 3" lengths. Fold each one in half to form a "V," and staple to the side of the tag. Use a glue dot or a dab of craft glue to attach the flower below the ribbons (see photo on previous page).

6. Thread a length of ribbon through the tag's hole and tie the tag onto the basket's handle.

7. Fill the basket with the items listed below (see photo on previous page). Feel free to add or substitute items as you deem necessary. Trial-size toiletries are readily available and will give the basket a true "hotel" look.

Estimated time: 15 minutes

Recommended Basket Fillers:

shampoo and conditioner, soap, toothpaste and new toothbrush, mouthwash, washcloths and hand towels, brush and comb, safety pins, bobby pins, needle and thread, map of your area, bottle of water and cups, small snack bags and/or fruit, newspaper or weekly magazine, toy or games, schedule of events (synagogue services, meal times, etc.)

I vividly remember crafting a beeswax havdalah candle in day camp when I was a kid. I loved the honey scent of the beeswax and rolling and braiding a havdalah candle for my family to use. I guess you can't mess with a classic, because a beeswax havdalah candle still comes to my mind when thinking about a havdalah craft.

havdalah candle

What you will need:

- ☐ waxed paper
- ☐ 3 sheets of beeswax in assorted colors
- ☐ scissors
- ☐ cotton wicks

How to do it:

1. Place a large sheet of waxed paper on your table or work surface. Working with one sheet of beeswax at a time, place the sheet of beeswax on the wax paper and use your knife or scissors to cut it across into three equal rectangles. Repeat with the other sheets of beeswax. For each braided candle you will use three different colors of wax rectangles.

2. Cut a piece of cotton wick 1" longer than your beeswax rectangle. Place the wick on top of the wax, with some of the wick sticking out of the top. Roll the wax up tightly between your palms until it forms a long candle. Press the top of the candle inwards so that the wick is secure. Repeat with the other two pieces of wax.

3. Braid the three candles together, holding them in your hands so that they don't become flattened (see photo on page 223). Pinch the bottom and top of the candle gently so that the braid is securely closed.

Estimated time: 15 minutes

The aromatic cloves used as besamim in the Havdalah ceremony are perfectly stored in this hand-decorated spice jar.

besamim box

- ☐ polymer oven bake clay in color(s) of your choice (we used Sculpey)
- ☐ small glass salt shaker
- ☐ plastic knife
- ☐ whole cloves
- ☐ glass beads, optional
- ☐ glue gun and glue sticks, optional

How to do it:

1. Roll the clay between your hands to soften it. Roll the clay into a ball and then flatten it into a rectangular shape as wide as the shaker is tall. If you underestimated the amount of clay you need, take more and reroll the ball with the additional clay before flattening it.

2. Remove the cover of the salt shaker and set aside. Press one end of the rectangle onto the shaker and wrap the clay around until it meets the other end. Press the two ends into each other. Pull and press the clay upward to the top of the shaker, then pull and press the clay down to the base of the shaker. (If you choose, you can use two different colors, as we did in the pictured project.)

3. Roll the shaker in your hands to release and pop any air bubbles and to smooth out the clay.

4. Place the shaker on its side and, with your knife, trim any excess clay from the top and bottom. Be sure that the cover is able to twist back on easily and that the edges are smooth.

5. Decorate the shaker by rolling and/or cutting out clay letters or shapes and pressing them onto the shaker.

6. Preheat oven to 275°F. Place the shaker into the oven and bake for 25 minutes. Do not remove from oven until it is completely cool.

Optional: Before baking shaker, press glass beads into the clay in the design of your choice. Please note: If beads fall off or are loose after baking, reattach with a glue gun and glue sticks.

Estimated time: 1 hour
Bake time: 25 minutes

SHABBAT KIDDUSH

Kiddush, the blessing recited over wine or grape juice on Shabbat, also refers to an enjoyable Shabbat day get-together. It is often held in shul or in someone's home right after the Shabbat morning services. The Kiddush celebration includes enjoying the delicacies that are served. A Kiddush is often held in honor of a happy occasion, but you don't really need an excuse to spend time with friends and family.

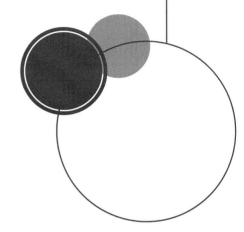

■ Set up:

A Kiddush is usually set up buffet-style so that it's simple for guests to serve themselves. Use large bowls to hold salad, and platters for the rest of the food. Ladle the cholent into individual crocks set on a tray before the Kiddush. This eliminates the mess of dishing out cholent during the Kiddush and will enable you to socialize with others. Place plates, napkins, and silverware in piles interspersed between the serving pieces along the buffet table.

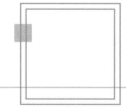

■ Food:

A Kiddush menu usually comprises traditional Shabbat-day recipes. Try our cholent recipe (page 230), served with a leafy green salad (page 231). For those who just want to nibble something sweet, there are chocolate chip cookies (page 234), black-n-white cake (page 232), and fruit skewers (page 206).

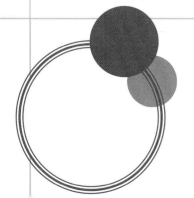

········ challah braiding ········

What you will need:

- ☐ sugar shaker
- ☐ pastry board
- ☐ sharp knife
- ☐ clean dish towel
- ☐ 4-6 oval challah baking pans, loaf pans or cookie sheets with parchment paper
- ☐ small bowl or custard cup
- ☐ fork or whisk
- ☐ pastry brush

Ingredients:

- ☐ ¼ cup flour
- ☐ 1 batch challah dough (see recipe on page 38)
- ☐ 1 egg
- ☐ sesame and/or poppy seeds, optional

On Shabbat we serve two loaves of challah to remind us of the two portions of manna that fell from the sky when the Jews were wandering in the desert. The manna didn't fall on Shabbat or Yom Tov; rather, two portions fell on the day before. Traditionally, this bread is braided, some say to represent the unity of the Jewish nation. Braiding a six-strand loaf of challah may seem daunting but it is certainly a craft that you can master — to paraphrase the Challah Maven, Devorah Heller, "Who said I'm not an artist or a sculptor? I can take a five-pound bag of flour and make something beautiful out of it." Nothing is as beautiful as a Shabbat challah.

How to do it:

1. Before you begin this intricate dough braid, place ¼ cup flour into a clean sugar shaker. Sprinkle the cutting board or counter with a dusting of flour.

2. Cut the dough into 4–6 equal pieces and work with one piece at a time. Cover the other pieces with a clean dish towel so they don't dry out. Cut the piece of dough into six equal pieces. (It is easier to cut it into thirds and then cut each piece in half.)

3. Sprinkle a dusting of flour onto each of the 6 pieces and roll them into ropes/strands. The strands should be between 10"–12" long, slightly wider in the middle and narrower at the ends.

4. Step A: Place the 6 dough ropes 1" apart on the work surface. Pinch the top of the ropes together. (Stand in front of the work surface; the baker is standing behind the board in the pictures in order to show the steps clearly.)

5. Label the ropes in your mind, starting with the outer rope on the right as number one. Push the 5th and 6th ropes on the left to the side.

6. Step B: Pick up strand number 3 from the right and place it above the other strands.

7. Step C: Cross strand 1 over strand 2.

8. Step D: Cross strand 4 over strand 1 and tighten the braid. Drop strand 3 between strands 4 and 1.

9. Step E: Working from the left, re-label the strands 1-6. Pick up strand 3 from the left, and place it above the other strands.

10. Step F: Cross strand 1 over strand 2.

11. Step G: Cross strand 4 over strand 1.

12. Step H: Drop strand 3 between strands 4 and 1.

13. Step I: Continue braiding in this manner, switching from right to left and back each time strand 3 is dropped in, numbering your strands on either left or right. Tighten the braid whenever you cross strand 4 over strand 1. You may need to stretch the strands as you get to the end of the braiding.

14. Step J: When you can no longer braid, tuck the loose ends under the braid. Pat the challah into shape and place into a loaf or oval challah baking pan; the pan will hold the shape and make the challah rise high. Alternatively, you can place the challah onto a cookie sheet covered with parchment paper; the challah will then be wider and flatter after baking.

15. Repeat for remaining dough.

16. Let rise in pan for 20 minutes–30 minutes.

17. Crack egg into a small bowl and beat until yolk and white are combined. Use a pastry brush to brush egg wash onto challot. Sprinkle on sesame or poppy seeds, if using.

18. Place the challot in oven and bake for 45 minutes. Check the challot to see if they are ready by tapping on the bottom. If the challot sound hollow and look dry, then they are done. Cool challot completely on a wire rack before storing in storage bags.

Estimated prep time: 20 minutes
Rising time: 20 minutes – 30 minutes
Bake time: 45 – 50 minutes
Parve • Yield: 4 large or 6 medium challahs

cholent

What you will need:

- [ ] crock pot or slow cooker
- [ ] peeler
- [ ] sharp knife and cutting board
- [ ] measuring cup and measuring spoons
- [ ] small strainer

Ingredients:

- [ ] 2 tablespoons vegetable oil
- [ ] 1 medium onion
- [ ] 6 medium potatoes
- [ ] 2 lbs. stew meat, flanken, or chuck steak
- [ ] ½ cup cholent bean mix or mix of navy, kidney, and pinto beans to make ½ cup beans
- [ ] ½ cup pearl barley
- [ ] ¼ cup ketchup
- [ ] ½ tablespoon kosher salt
- [ ] ⅛ teaspoon black pepper
- [ ] ½ tablespoon paprika
- [ ] 2 teaspoons garlic powder or 2 cloves fresh garlic, crushed
- [ ] 6-7 cups water

Cholent (see photo on page 225) is a type of stew that is eaten on Shabbat day by most Ashkenazi Jews. It is cooked before Shabbat and continues cooking over a low heat until the Shabbat-day meal is served. I like to cook the cholent in a crock pot because it cooks evenly and I don't have to worry about it burning.

How to do it:

1. Four to six hours prior to the onset of Shabbat, turn the crock pot to the high setting. Pour the vegetable oil into the crock pot. Peel the onion and use the sharp knife to dice it into small pieces. Place the diced onion into the crock pot.

2. Peel the potatoes, wash them, and cut them into chunks. Place the potatoes and meat into the crock pot.

3. Place the beans and barley into the strainer. Look for and discard any stones or shriveled beans. Rinse well under running water.

4. Pour the beans and barley into the crock pot and add the rest of the ingredients.

5. Cook on high for 4–6 hours. Before Shabbat, turn crock pot to low setting. Check to make sure that there is enough water in the cholent. There should be approximately one inch of water over top of the ingredients; if it looks too dry, add 1–2 cups of boiling water.

Estimated prep time: 20 minutes
Bake time: 6 hours
Meat • Yield: 8 servings

⋯⋯⋯ tossed salad ⋯⋯⋯

What you will need:

- ☐ colander or strainer
- ☐ large salad bowl or platter
- ☐ sharp knife and cutting board
- ☐ small bowl
- ☐ measuring cup
- ☐ measuring spoons
- ☐ fork or whisk

Ingredients:

- ☐ 1 head romaine lettuce and/or endive
- ☐ 1 avocado
- ☐ ½ pint grape tomatoes
- ☐ 2 scallions
- ☐ ¼ cup walnut or olive oil
- ☐ 1 lemon
- ☐ 2 teaspoons kosher salt, or to taste
- ☐ ¼ teaspoon pepper
- ☐ ½ cup toasted chopped nuts

This bright and refreshing salad is a sure crowd-pleaser and a cinch to toss together!

How to do it:

1. Wash lettuce well and drain in a colander. Tear lettuce into bite-size pieces and place into the bowl or on the platter.

2. Using the knife and cutting board, peel and slice the avocado and place on top of the lettuce. Cut the grape tomatoes in half. Slice the white part of the scallions. Place prepared tomatoes and scallions into the salad.

3. Pour the oil into the small bowl. Cut the lemon in half and squeeze into the oil; be careful to keep the pits out. Mix in the salt and pepper and stir very well with a fork or whisk.

4. Pour the dressing over the salad. If the salad is in the bowl, toss well. If the salad is on a platter, drizzle the dressing over the vegetables.

5. Sprinkle the nuts over the salad before serving.

Estimated time: 15 minutes
Parve • Yield: 6 – 8 servings

black-n-white cake

What you will need:

- [ ] 10-cup bundt pan
- [ ] cooking spray
- [ ] large bowl
- [ ] electric mixer
- [ ] measuring cups and spoons
- [ ] liquid measuring cup
- [ ] spatula
- [ ] knife
- [ ] 2 small bowls
- [ ] 2 spoons

Cake Ingredients:

- [ ] 3 cups flour
- [ ] 2 teaspoons baking powder
- [ ] ½ teaspoon salt
- [ ] 1 cup oil
- [ ] 1½ cups sugar
- [ ] 3 eggs
- [ ] 1 teaspoon vanilla extract
- [ ] 1 teaspoon almond extract
- [ ] 1 cup water
- [ ] ¾ cup chocolate syrup
- [ ] ½ teaspoon baking soda

Icing Ingredients:

- [ ] 1 cup confectioners' sugar
- [ ] 1-2 tablespoon soy milk
- [ ] ½ teaspoon vanilla extract OR 2 tablespoons cocoa

This cake is soft and delicious and looks so appealing. My family calls it "Sara's black-n-white cake" because my friend Sara gave me the recipe. Bake it early on Friday — everyone will enjoy a slice when they take a break on this hectic day.

How to do it:

1. Preheat the oven to 350°F. Spray the bundt pan with cooking spray and set aside.

2. Place flour, baking powder, and salt into a large bowl; mix lightly. Set aside.

3. Place the oil and sugar into the mixer bowl and mix on a medium-high setting. Add the eggs, one at a time, and continue mixing until the mixture is light and fluffy. Add the vanilla and almond extracts.

4. Turn mixer speed to low and add some of the flour mixture, then some of the water, then more flour, then the rest of the water, and then the rest of the flour mixture. Mix until all the batter ingredients are combined.

5. Pour ⅔ of the batter into the prepared pan.

6. Add the chocolate syrup and baking soda to the remaining ⅓ of the batter and mix it well with your spatula.

7. Pour the chocolate batter over the white batter. Use a knife to "cut" the chocolate batter into the white batter.

8. Place in oven and bake for 1 hour.

9. Remove the cake from the oven and allow to cool for 15 minutes. Turn the cake out onto a cake plate. If it's hard to lift off the pan, use a spatula or knife to loosen the cake from the sides. Allow cake to cool completely.

10. For white icing: In a small bowl, mix together 1 cup confectioner's sugar, 1 tablespoon soy milk, and vanilla extract. For chocolate icing, use cocoa instead of vanilla. If the icing is too thick, add soy milk, a bit at a time.

11. Use a spoon to drizzle the white icing all around the cake. Then drizzle the chocolate icing all around.

Estimated prep time: 25 – 30 minutes
Bake time: 1 hour
Cooling time: 1 hour
Parve • Yield: 12 servings

········ best-ever chocolate chip cookies ········

What you will need:

- ☐ knife
- ☐ small microwave-safe bowl
- ☐ medium mixing bowl
- ☐ large mixing bowl
- ☐ large spoon
- ☐ measuring cups and spoons
- ☐ plastic wrap
- ☐ 2 baking sheets
- ☐ parchment paper
- ☐ wire rack

Ingredients:

- ☐ 1 cup (2 sticks) butter or margarine
- ☐ 2 cups flour
- ☐ ½ teaspoon salt
- ☐ ½ teaspoon baking soda
- ☐ 1 cup dark-brown sugar
- ☐ ½ cup sugar
- ☐ 1 extra-large egg
- ☐ ½ tablespoon vanilla
- ☐ 1⅓ cups chocolate chips
- ☐ 1 cup sweetened shredded coconut or chopped walnuts

There are loads of chocolate chip cookie recipes around, but after tasting these you will know why I call them "best ever"! They are just the best chocolate chip cookies you've ever tasted and they are so easy to make — just mix them by hand in a large bowl! No mixer needed for this super-simple recipe.

How to do it:

1. Cut the butter or margarine into 1" pieces and place into the small microwave-safe bowl. Microwave for 1–2 minutes until butter is melted; cool.

2. Place the flour, salt, and baking soda into the medium mixing bowl; mix with a large spoon to combine.

3. Pour the cooled butter or margarine into the large mixing bowl. Add the brown sugar, white sugar, egg, and vanilla. Mix well.

4. Slowly beat in the flour mixture by hand. When it is completely incorporated, gently fold in the chocolate chips and shredded coconut.

5. Cover the bowl with plastic wrap and place in the fridge for 30 minutes.

6. While the dough is chilling, preheat the oven to 350°F and cover the baking sheets with parchment paper.

7. Drop tablespoonfuls of the chilled cookie dough onto the prepared baking sheets. Leave a 1" space between cookies because they will spread during baking. Place the baking sheets into the preheated oven and bake for 12–14 minutes.

8. Remove from oven. Let cookies cool for one minute on the baking sheets; remove to a wire rack to finish cooling.

Estimated prep time: 15 minutes
Chill time: 30 minutes
Bake time: 12 – 14 minutes
Dairy or Parve • Yield: 40 cookies

FOR EVERY DAY

Sure, crafting is one of the best ways to get into the spirit of an upcoming holiday. But why wait for a holiday to get the creative juices flowing? The projects in this section are perfect for those times when you want to make something special for no special reason. If you have some free time during summer vacation or are stuck at home on a cold winter's day, get out your glue gun, paper and scissors, and any other craft supplies you may need — and have some fun!

These projects are perfect for all year 'round because they can be made at any time and are open to endless variations. They also make wonderful birthday and special-occasion gifts. For added enjoyment, gather a friend or two and craft together.

Let your imagination soar — and happy crafting!

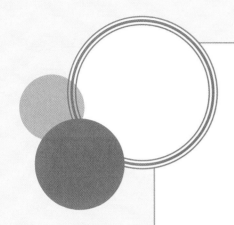

Picture frames are the perfect craft medium because you can decorate them in countless ways. They can be painted, decoupaged, or antiqued. Adding stickers, trim, tags, ribbons, and flowers results in an original picture-frame project.

Decorating picture frames is an inexpensive and fun birthday party project. Prepare an assortment of paint colors, papers, stickers, and embellishments, enabling each partygoer to craft his or her "picture perfect" masterpiece.

embellished picture frame

What you will need:

- ☐ unfinished wood craft frame
- ☐ scrapbook paper
- ☐ sandpaper
- ☐ paper towels
- ☐ 2 (1"-wide) foam brushes
- ☐ acrylic paint in the color(s) of your choice
- ☐ pencil
- ☐ scissors
- ☐ decoupage medium, such as Mod Podge
- ☐ 1"-wide bristle paintbrush
- ☐ embellishments: assortment of alphabet stickers, ribbon, trim, flowers, stickers, tags
- ☐ double-sided adhesive tape, or glue gun and glue sticks

How to do it:

1. Disassemble the frame and set the frame back and glass away from the crafting area.

2. Place the scrapbook paper facedown on the work surface in front of you. Place the frame on top of it and trace the outside of the frame and the frame opening onto the back of the paper. Set paper aside.

3. Take the sandpaper and sand down any rough edges of the picture frame. Use a damp paper towel to brush off any dust.

4. Using a foam brush, paint the inside and outside edges and corners of the frame with acrylic paint. Place to the side and let dry.

5. Meanwhile, cut the outlined frame from the scrapbook paper.

6. Use a clean foam brush to apply a thin coat of Mod Podge to the front of frame. Press on the traced paper frame. Use your fingers to smooth out any air bubbles. Let dry.

7. Sand the edges of the paper lightly to smooth rough edges.

8. Take a dry bristle paintbrush and dab a small amount of paint (in a coordinating color) onto the bristles. Stroke the paint lightly around the frame's inner and outer edges. Let dry.

9. Use a clean foam brush to stroke on a second coat of Mod Podge over the entire frame.

10. Decorate the frame by sticking on embellishments with double-sided adhesive tape or glue gun. Reassemble frame.

Estimated time: 45 minutes

Drying time: approxmately 4 hours, divided

This oversized clipboard is wonderfully convenient for keeping all your papers in one place. Hang it on the wall or leave it on your desk for ready access.

oversized clipboard

What you will need:

☐ tape runner or double-sided adhesive tape

☐ 2 (12"x12") sheets cardstock in coordinating colors

☐ oversized clipboard, (we used ProvoCraft)

☐ pencil and ruler

☐ soda/water bottle cap

☐ scissors

☐ marker

☐ glue gun and glue sticks

☐ 3 ribbons in colors coordinating with the paper

☐ buttons, tags, or charms

☐ rub-on letters or alphabet sticker

☐ 4 photo corners, optional

☐ photograph, optional

How to do it:

1. Use the tape runner to glue one sheet of cardstock to the clipboard, centering the paper underneath the large clip.

2. Cut 4"-wide strip of paper from the second piece of cardstock. On the back of the cardstock, toward the edge, repeatedly trace around the bottle cap with a pencil. The circles should be close together, going across the entire bottom edge of the paper to form the outline for the scalloped edge.

3. Cut around the outer edges of the circles to create a scalloped edge (see photo).

4. Use a marker to outline the scallop on the front of the cardstock.

5. With the tape runner, glue the scalloped cardstock onto the clipboard, 1" below the first piece of cardstock.

6. Affix rub-on or sticker initials on the left of the scalloped paper.

7. Use glue gun and glue sticks and/or double-sided adhesive tape to attach ribbons to the top and bottom of the clipboard. Attach buttons and tags as well. (Don't attach embellishments to the clipboard center because they will make the surface difficult to write on.)

8. Thread approximately 5" length of ribbon through the hole in the clip and knot to secure. Trim ribbon edges.

9. Thread a longer piece of ribbon through the hole in the clip. Tie to secure. Tie a pen to the free end of the ribbon.

Optional: Personalize the clipboard by attaching a photo on the right hand side (see photo). Use a tape runner to attach photo corners to each corner and attach to clipboard cover.

Estimated time: 45 minutes–1 hour

Decorate this fabulous mirror to match your room. As an added bonus, tie the ribbon bow extra long; use the tails for holding loads of hair clips.

decorated mirror

What you will need:

- ☐ 12"x12" finished wood framed mirror
- ☐ 12"x12" scrapbook paper
- ☐ pencil and ruler
- ☐ scissors
- ☐ 1"-wide foam brush
- ☐ decoupage medium, such as Mod Podge
- ☐ brown stamp pad
- ☐ chipboard flower stickers
- ☐ small buttons
- ☐ 1½" alphabet stickers
- ☐ 1-2 yards of ¾"-1"-wide ribbon
- ☐ craft glue ,or glue gun and glue sticks

How to do it:

1. Disassemble the mirror and set the mirror and backing away from the crafting area.

2. With the pencil, trace the mirror opening onto the back of the scrapbook paper and cut out with scissors.

3. With a foam brush, brush a thin coat of Mod Podge onto the front of the frame.

4. Carefully place the cut-out scrapbook paper onto the coated frame and smooth out any air bubbles. Let dry.

5. Gently press the stamp pad around the inner and outer edges of the frame.

6. Brush another thin coat of Mod Podge on top of the scrapbook paper and let dry completely.

7. Attach the chipboard flower stickers and buttons to the top left-hand side of the frame, using a glue gun and glue sticks if necessary (see photo).

8. Reassemble the mirror.

9. Fold the wide ribbon in half. Make a bow at the center. Turn the mirror over and use craft glue, or a glue gun and glue sticks, to adhere the bow's tails to the back of the mirror.

10. Hang the mirror using the sawtooth hangers attached to the back of the frame. Affix a nail to the wall a few inches above the center of the mirror and place the bow over the nail. Tighten the bow if necessary.

Estimated time: 45 minutes
Drying time: 3 hours, divided

These versatile bookends will keep order on your bookshelf in a fun, personalized way. You can craft them to match the desk for a unified look. We used unfinished wooden elements manufactured by Darice, purchased at Michael's.

built-by-me bookends

What you will need:

- [ ] wooden initial 7"-9" high
- [ ] 2 or more sheets coordinating patterned scrapbook paper
- [ ] ruler and pencil
- [ ] unfinished grooved wooden bookends
- [ ] unfinished wooden picture frame (5"x7" frame to hold 4"x6" picture)
- [ ] sandpaper
- [ ] paper towel
- [ ] acrylic paint
- [ ] 2 (1") paintbrushes
- [ ] scissors
- [ ] decoupage medium, such as Mod Podge
- [ ] spray adhesive, optional
- [ ] glue gun and glue sticks
- [ ] alphabet sticker or rub-on
- [ ] chipboard tag
- [ ] 2 (10" length) ribbons
- [ ] chipboard shapes, glue runner, optional

How to do it:

1. Disassemble the picture frame and set the frame back and glass away from the crafting area.

2. With a pencil, trace the wooden initial onto the back of a scrapbook paper. Trace the fronts of the frame and of each bookend onto the backs of additional sheets of paper. Set aside.

3. Sand all the edges of the bookends, frame, and initial until smooth. Wipe away shavings and dust with a damp paper towel.

4. Use the acrylic paint and a brush to paint pieces. Let dry.

5. Use scissors to cut out the outlined shapes.

6. Place the initial, bookends, and front of frame on a work surface in a well-ventilated area. Coat the surface of each piece with a thin layer of Mod Podge or spray a light coat of adhesive on the front of each wooden piece, following manufacturer's instructions.

7. Adhere a cut-out paper shape to each wooden piece and smooth out any air bubbles. Let dry. Sand edges smooth.

8. Use a paintbrush to brush a thin coat of Mod Podge onto the front of each piece. Let dry.

9. Hot glue the bottom of the initial into the groove of one bookend. Reassemble the frame; insert photo and glue the bottom of the frame into the groove of the other bookend.

10. Attach an alphabet sticker or rub-on to the tag. Tie ribbons around the top of the initial, with the tag knotted into the center.

Optional: Trace chipboard shapes onto the backs of leftover scraps of paper. Cut out; attach the paper shapes to the chipboard with a glue runner. Use the glue gun to adhere the shapes to the frame.

Estimated time: 1 hour

Total drying time: 4–8 hours, divided

Fulfill the mitzvah of placing the words of the Shema on your doorpost by inserting your mezuzah (a parchment scroll on which a scribe has written the words of Shema) into this beautiful case and affixing it to a doorway of your home.

mezuzah

What you will need:

☐ lucite or clear plastic mezuzah case

☐ E6000 adhesive

☐ paper plate

☐ small sea glass or stained glass shards (with rounded edges) (we used 1 package of Cobblets, sold in the stained glass section of Michael's)

How to do it:

1. Remove the back of the mezuzah case and place away from your crafting area.

2. Place the mezuzah case, face up, on a paper plate. Working with one small area of the case at a time, cover that space with a thick layer of E6000. Press the Cobblets into the glue. If there is a ש on the mezuzah case, take care not to cover it with glue and Cobblets.

3. After the mezuzah case is decorated, let dry for 24 hours before hanging. Place the mezuzah scroll into the case, replace the back, and hang. Consult your rabbi about the proper method of hanging a mezuzah.

Estimated time: 30 minutes
Drying time: 4–24 hours

The great part of directing craft workshops in Camp Hedvah is that I receive instant feedback. When the girls "ooh and aah" over a craft they think is cool, I know it's a winner. I really know that I have hit upon a wonderful craft when even staff members all begin requesting a particular project. This is just such a craft — everyone wants it!

candy pillow

What you will need:

- ☐ fabric remnant
- ☐ pinking shears
- ☐ needle and thread or sewing machine
- ☐ 2 rubber bands or narrow ponytail holders
- ☐ polyester fiberfill or bolster pillow
- ☐ 3 (¼"–⅜"-wide) yards polyester grosgrain ribbon in assorted colors, cut into 1-yard lengths
- ☐ wooden dowels and clothespins or metal alligator clips
- ☐ cookie sheet or large baking pan
- ☐ aluminum foil

How to do it:

1. If using fiberfill, use pinking shears to cut the fabric into a rectangle approximately 21"x24". If using a bolster pillow, cut the fabric 6-8 inches longer and 2 inches wider than the pillow.

2. Fold fabric in half, widthwise, right side (printed side) facing in.

3. Use the needle and thread or sewing machine to sew the edges together along the width, forming a tube with open ends.

4. Turn tube right-side-out. Grasp it 3-4 inches from one end and wrap a rubber band tightly around it to form the "wrapper's" twist.

5. Stuff the fiberfill into the the tube, packing tightly so that it is not lumpy. Do not stuff the last 3-4 inches of the tube. (If using a bolster pillow, stuff it into the tube and continue to step 6.)

6. To close the open end, wrap a rubber band tightly around it and fluff the fabric out at both ends.

7. For ribbon curls: Preheat the oven to 250°F. Cover a cookie sheet with aluminum foil and set aside.

8. With a clothespin, clip one end of each cut ribbon to a dowel. Wind the ribbon tightly around the dowel, making sure not to overlap the ribbon. Clip the ribbon end to the dowel to secure.

9. Place wrapped dowels onto the cookie sheet. Bake for 20 minutes. Turn oven off and let cool 20 minutes before removing dowels.

10. When dowels have cooled, unwrap ribbon. If curls are not tight, rewrap, return to oven, and bake for 10 more minutes. Cut each ribbon curl in half. Tie around the rubber bands to cover them.

Estimated time: 1 hour
Bake time (for ribbon curls): 20-30 minutes
Cooling time: 40 minutes, divided

I love scrapbooking! I think it's a marvelous way to save and share your memories. This scrapbook craft is a magnificent way to display your family's photos for all to see. Photos can be attached to both sides of the frame. You can place it on a table, desk, bookcase, or mantel for everyone to enjoy.

If your family has loads of pictures, then choosing the right ones may be the hardest part of the project, so make a few! These also make wonderful gifts; customize them with the right word or phrase to fit the pictures.

scrapbook frame

What you will need:

- [ ] 6 or more chipboard lacing cards (we used Cosmo Cricket)
- [ ] 12"x12" scrapbook paper in colors and patterns of your choice
- [ ] pencil
- [ ] scissors and/or paper cutter
- [ ] glue stick
- [ ] hole puncher or Crop-a-dile
- [ ] sandpaper
- [ ] stickers and embellishments
- [ ] chipboard, sticker, or die-cut letters
- [ ] double-sided adhesive foam dots and/or 3-D self-adhesive foam dots
- [ ] ribbon, approximately 1 yard to connect every 2 cards (we used 5 yards)

How to do it:

1. Trace the chipboard cards onto the backs of the scrapbook papers. Cut out the traced card shapes with the paper cutter or scissors. You will need 1 card and 2 cut-out shapes for each letter of the word you choose.

2. Use your glue stick to glue the scrapbook paper onto the front and back of each card.

3. Use hole puncher or Crop-a-dile to reopen the lacing holes on the edges of the chipboard cards.

4. Use the sandpaper to rub around the front and back edges of each of the prepared chipboard cards so that you see the inner white part of the paper.

5. Glue pictures to the front and back of each card, trimming pictures if necessary. Glue on embellishments and stickers with the self-adhesive foam dots, or use 3-D self-adhesive foam dots to make embellishments pop out. Attach a letter to each card to spell out the word FAMILY or another word of your choice.

6. Lace one chipboard card to another with the the ribbons. Knot ribbon or tie into a bow and trim the ends when you have finished lacing. Repeat, lacing the other cards until they are all attached.

7. Thread ribbon through the holes of either end of your display. Tie a bow or knot and trim off excess ribbon.

Estimated time: 1 hour

If your desk, like mine, is stuck in a perpetual state of messiness, then this desk set is just the project for you. Finally, you'll have a neat way to store the pens, pencils, papers, and other junk that seems to multiply and take over your desk space. With such attractive organizing accessories that you've crafted yourself out of basic household items, you'll be tempted to keep everything in its place — I'm certainly hoping that will happen to me!

desk set

What you will need:

- [ ] assorted clean metal, cardboard, or plastic containers
- [ ] scrapbooking or wrapping paper
- [ ] ruler and pencil
- [ ] scissors
- [ ] foam brush
- [ ] decoupage medium, such as Mod Podge
- [ ] spray adhesive, optional
- [ ] X-Acto knife
- [ ] sandpaper
- [ ] decorative trim
- [ ] glue gun and glue sticks
- [ ] alphabet stickers
- [ ] paper embellishments, optional

How to do it:

1. Measure the height and width of each container and, with a pencil, mark the measurements, plus ½" for overlapping, onto the back of the paper. Cut out the measured paper.

2. Use the foam brush to coat the front surface of each piece with a thin layer of Mod Podge or spray a light coat of adhesive on the front of each container, following manufacturer's instructions. Smooth out any air bubbles with your fingers. Let dry.

3. Use an X-Acto knife to trim any excess paper from the top and/or bottom of the container.

4. Use sandpaper to sand all the edges of the paper coverings.

5. Brush another coat of Mod Podge over the paper. Let dry.

6. Optional: Cut a piece of decorative trim to fit around the top circumference of the container and attach with a glue gun and glue sticks.

7. Label the container by spelling out the names of the item(s) with alphabet stickers. Use paper embellishments if desired.

Estimated time: 30 minutes
Drying time: 1–2 hours, divided

Keep all your important papers, pictures and fun stuff tacked up for easy access and on display on a funky bulletin board made from an embellished picture frame (see photo, page 238)! It's a great addition to your desk set. Maximize your time by crafting the pushpins while the bulletin board dries, or attach strong circular magnets instead of pushpins (see photo on previous page).

bulletin board and pushpins

What you will need:

Bulletin Board:

- ☐ embellished picture frame, page 238
- ☐ ruler and pencil
- ☐ 8½"x11" sheet foam core board
- ☐ sharp scissors or X-Acto knife
- ☐ roll of corkboard material
- ☐ craft glue
- ☐ 2"-wide foam brush
- ☐ acrylic paint in the color of your choice

Pushpins:

- ☐ flat marbles
- ☐ patterned paper
- ☐ pencil
- ☐ scissors or circle punch
- ☐ E6000 adhesive
- ☐ toothpick
- ☐ flat pushpins

How to do it:

Bulletin Board:

1. Remove the glass and back of the frame and place out of crafting area. With the ruler and pencil, measure the frame's opening and mark the measurements onto the foam core. Cut out the rectangle with scissors or X-Acto knife.

2. Unroll the corkboard on a flat surface. Place the cut-out rectangle on top and trace onto the cork. Cut out the cork rectangle.

3. Spread craft glue onto the foam core rectangle and attach the cork. Smooth with your fingers to eliminate air bubbles. If the cork curls upward, place several heavy books on top while glue dries. Let dry 1-2 hours.

4. Use a foam brush to paint the cork the color of your choice. Let dry.

5. Place the cork-covered foam core into the frame opening and replace frame back. Reserve frame glass for another use.

Pushpins:

1. For each pushpin: place the marble on the back of the patterned paper and trace around it with a pencil.

2. Cut out the shape with scissors or a circle punch.

3. Squeeze a dab of E6000 onto a paper scrap. With a toothpick, transfer a drop of the E6000 to the paper circle and place the marble on the paper. Press out any air bubbles and let dry.

4. Use E6000 to glue a pushpin to the marble's flat side and let dry.

Estimated time: 1 hour

Drying time: 2–4 hours

Templates

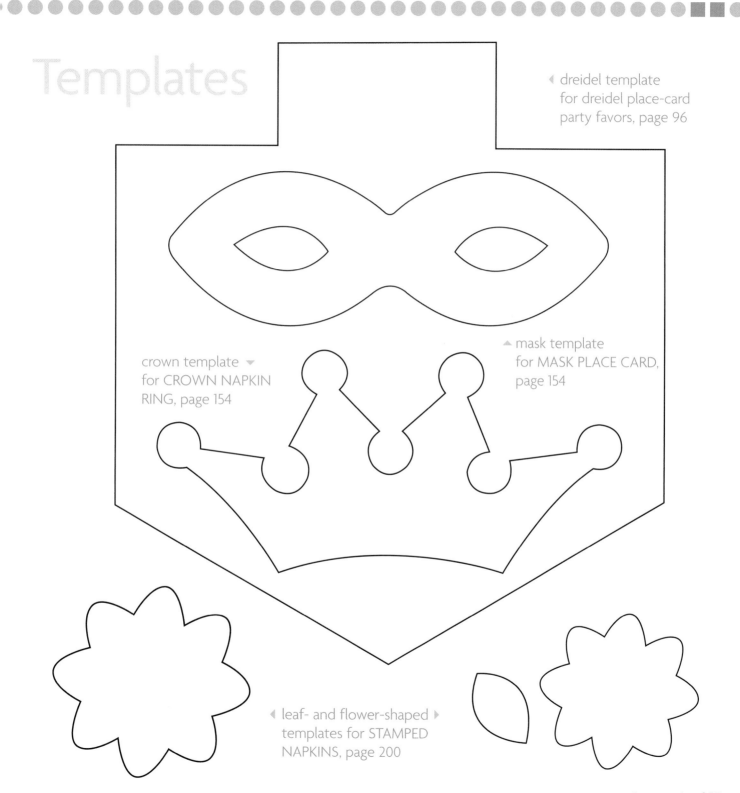

dreidel template
for dreidel place-card
party favors, page 96

▲ mask template
for MASK PLACE CARD,
page 154

crown template ▼
for CROWN NAPKIN
RING, page 154

◄ leaf- and flower-shaped ►
templates for STAMPED
NAPKINS, page 200

◄ leek or cabbage	◄ apple	שֶׁתִּתְחַדֵּשׁ עָלֵינוּ שָׁנָה טוֹבָה וּמְתוּקָה
שֶׁיִּכָּרְתוּ שׂוֹנְאֵינוּ		

שֶׁיִּכָּרְתוּ שׂוֹנְאֵינוּ

◄ fenugreek or carrots
שֶׁיִּרְבּוּ זְכִיּוֹתֵינוּ

◄ beets
שֶׁיִּסְתַּלְּקוּ אוֹיְבֵינוּ

◄ pomegranate
שֶׁנִּרְבֶּה זְכִיּוֹת כְּרִמּוֹן

◄ head of sheep or fish
שֶׁנִּהְיֶה לְרֹאשׁ וְלֹא לְזָנָב

◄ fish
שֶׁנִּפְרֶה וְנִרְבֶּה כְּדָגִים

◄ gourd
שֶׁיִּקָּרַע גְּזַר דִּינֵנוּ וְיִקָּרְאוּ לְפָנֶיךָ זְכִיּוֹתֵינוּ

Hebrew *Yehi Ratzon* ▲ ►
templates for
SIMAN MARKERS,
page 30

◄ dates
שֶׁיִּתַּמּוּ שׂוֹנְאֵינוּ

apple ▶

... that You renew for us
a good and sweet year

leek or cabbage ▶

... that our enemies
be decimated

fenugreek or carrots ▶

... that our merits increase

beets ▶

... that our adversaries
be removed

pomegranate ▶

... that our merits increase as
[the seeds of] a pomegranate

head of sheep or fish ▶

... that we be as the head
and not as the tail

fish ▶

... that we be fruitful
and multiply like fish

gourd ▶

... that the decree of our
sentence be torn asunder;
and may our merits
be proclaimed before You

dates ▶

... that our enemies
be consumed

◀ ▲ English *Yehi Ratzon*
templates for
SIMAN MARKERS,
page 30

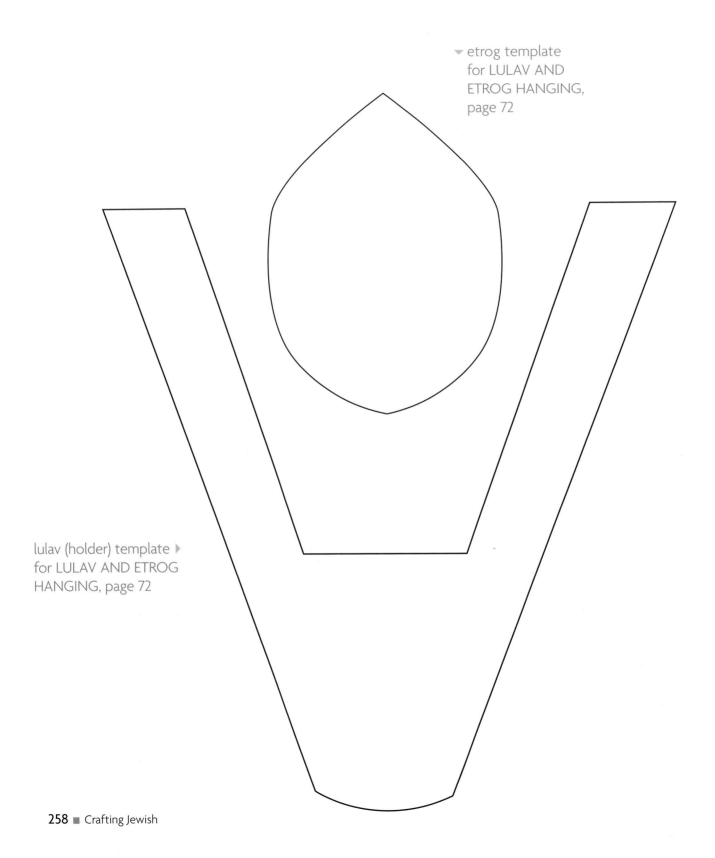

etrog template
for LULAV AND
ETROG HANGING,
page 72

lulav (holder) template ▶
for LULAV AND ETROG
HANGING, page 72

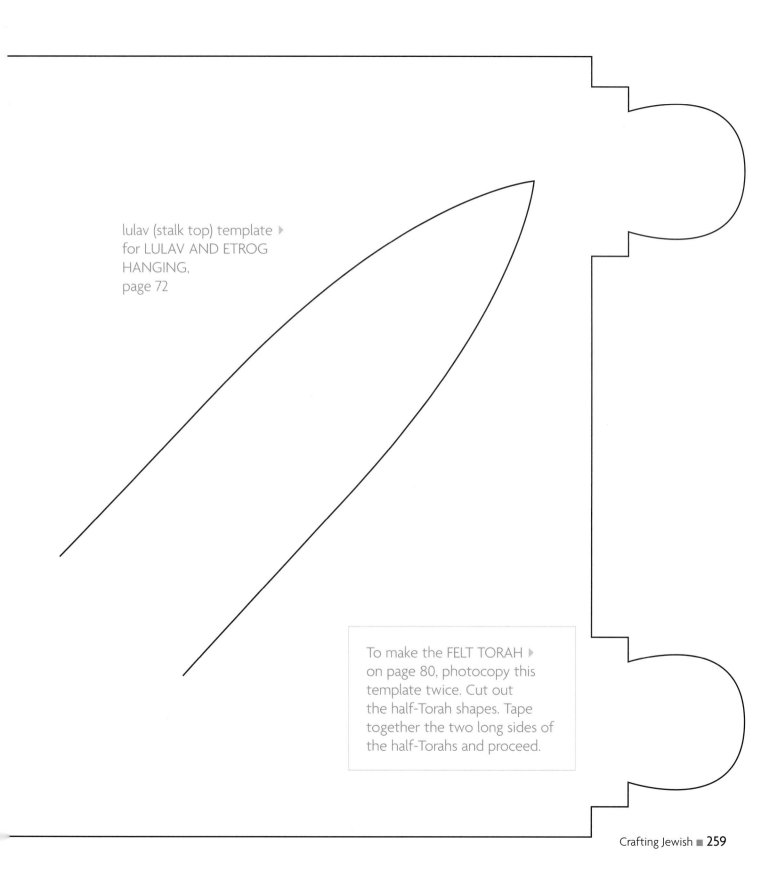

lulav (stalk top) template ▶
for LULAV AND ETROG
HANGING,
page 72

To make the FELT TORAH ▶
on page 80, photocopy this
template twice. Cut out
the half-Torah shapes. Tape
together the two long sides of
the half-Torahs and proceed.

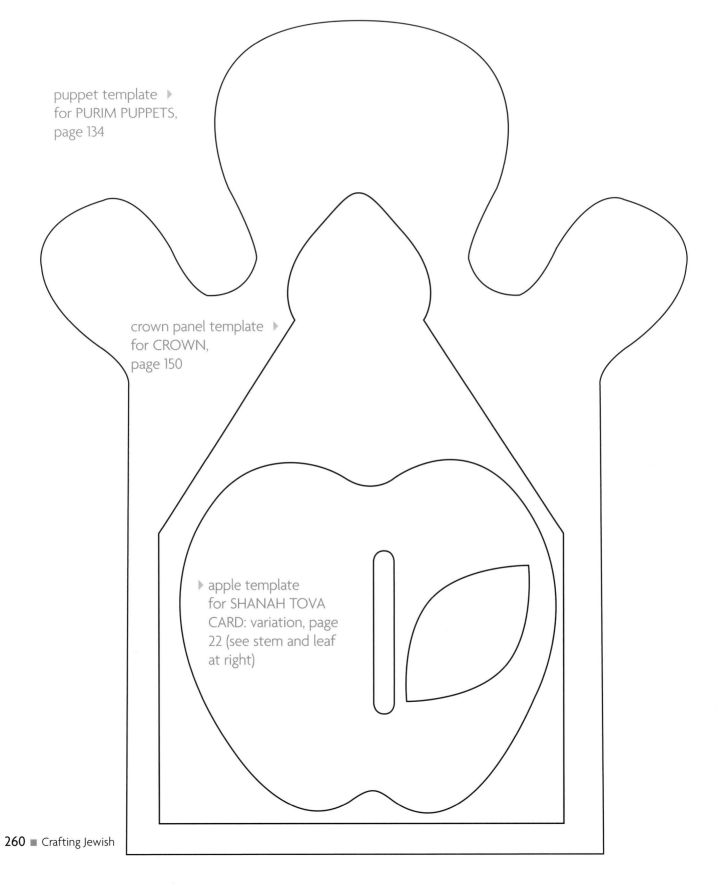

puppet template ▶
for PURIM PUPPETS,
page 134

crown panel template ▶
for CROWN,
page 150

▶ apple template
for SHANAH TOVA
CARD: variation, page
22 (see stem and leaf
at right)

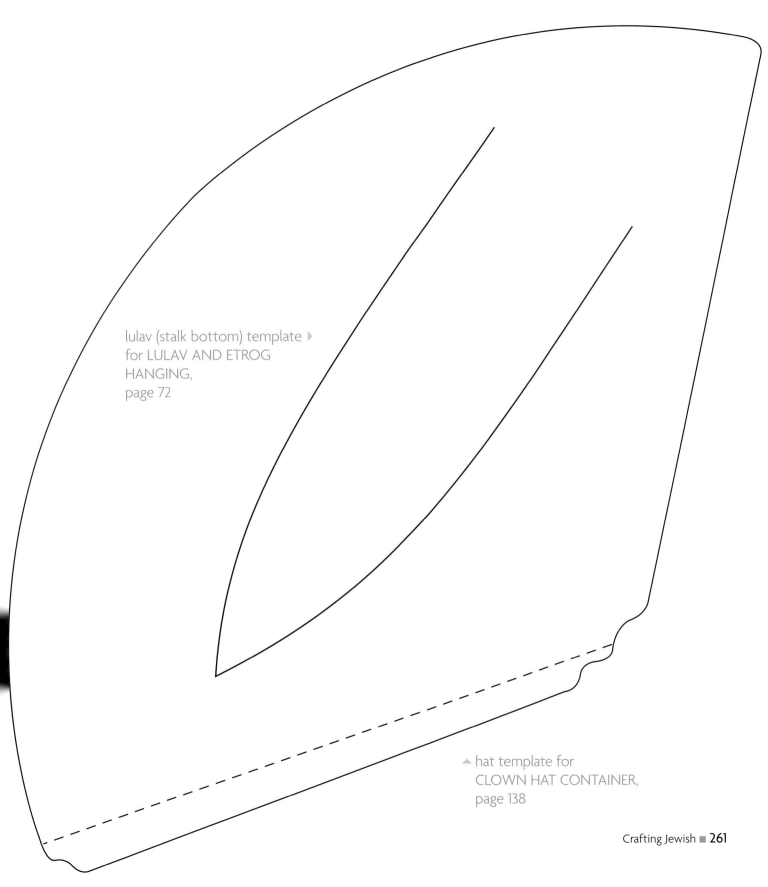

lulav (stalk bottom) template ▷
for LULAV AND ETROG
HANGING,
page 72

▲ hat template for
CLOWN HAT CONTAINER,
page 138

matzo

Matzo word and design template, for MATZO TRAY, page 174

Torah template for "STAINED GLASS" FLAG, page 78

CLEANING FOR PESACH CHECKLIST

LIVING ROOM/FAMILY ROOM
- ☐ Couch
- ☐ Chairs
- ☐ Side table(s)
- ☐ Coffee table
- ☐ Cabinets/bookshelves
- ☐ Books and games
- ☐ _____
- ☐ _____

DINING ROOM
- ☐ Table
- ☐ Chairs
- ☐ Buffet/sideboard
- ☐ Cabinetry
- ☐ Serving ware
- ☐ _____
- ☐ _____

KITCHEN
- ☐ Table
- ☐ Chairs
- ☐ Cabinets and drawers
- ☐ Pantry
- ☐ Dishes
- ☐ Flatware and cutlery
- ☐ Pots and pans
- ☐ Mixer
- ☐ Food processor
- ☐ Toaster
- ☐ Oven
- ☐ Stove
- ☐ Microwave
- ☐ Refrigerator and freezer
- ☐ Sinks
- ☐ Dish washer
- ☐ Garbage disposal
- ☐ _____
- ☐ _____

BEDROOM(S)
- ☐ Bed
- ☐ Closet
- ☐ Night table
- ☐ Under the bed
- ☐ Desk
- ☐ Dresser drawers
- ☐ Bookshelf and books
- ☐ Wastebasket
- ☐ _____

BATHROOM(S)
- ☐ Vanity
- ☐ Medicine cabinet
- ☐ Wastebasket
- ☐ _____

PLAYROOM
- ☐ Toy box
- ☐ Closet and sheves
- ☐ Toys
- ☐ Games and puzzles
- ☐ Table and chairs
- ☐ _____

GARAGE
- ☐ Car
- ☐ Car seat
- ☐ Stroller
- ☐ Outdoor toys
- ☐ _____

MISCELLANEOUS
- ☐ Pocketbooks and purses
- ☐ Backpacks and briefcases
- ☐ Telephones and computer(s)
- ☐ Vacuum cleaner and brooms
- ☐ Garbage cans
- ☐ _____
- ☐ _____

TO MAKE A BLANKET STITCH:

Insert needle through back of the fabric to the front at 1. Push needle back through fabric from the front at 2, leaving a bit of slack in the thread (this stitch will form a diagonal line). Push the needle through from the back at 3. Catch the diagonal thread under the needle, bringing the diagonal thread down to the level of 1 again (it will form an "L" shape); tighten the thread. Push the needle through to the back again at 4. Repeat the blanket stitch as necessary.

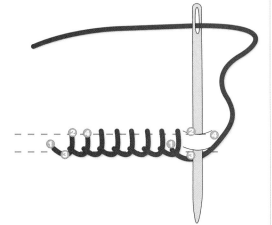

TO MAKE A RUNNING STITCH:

From the back, bring the needle up through the fabric to the front. Insert the needle through the fabric to the back and up again a short distance away. The space between the stitches should be half the length of the stitches themselves. Keeping the stitches even, repeat as many times as needed. You will have a line of stitches with a slight separation between them.

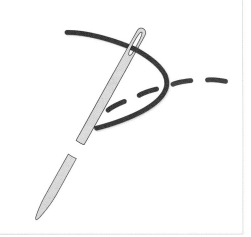

TO MAKE A BACKSTITCH:

Pull thread through from the back to the front. Push needle back to reverse side of fabric through the same hole where the first stitch ends. Come back out on the front, keeping the stitches the same size. This forms a line of very closely spaced stitches.

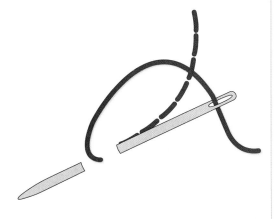

אבגגדדההו

זחטיככלל

מנסעפ

צקרשת

Resources

CRAFT SUPPLIES Having the right supplies is always important, whether you are crafting, cooking, or setting up a party. These stores and/or companies are the places we turn to for all our supply needs. Check out your local craft, notions, and housewares stores, as well, for some great stuff that the big chain stores don't carry. These crafting retail chains carry most of the items used in this book.

A.C. MOORE: Offering a vast selection of arts, crafts, and floral merchandise with stores located throughout eastern U.S. (acmoore.com)

AMAZING SAVINGS: Crazy low prices on name-brand scrapbooking and craft supplies. (amazingsavings.com)

HOBBY LOBBY: The place to shop for crafting and scrapbooking supplies with stores throughout southern and midwestern U.S. (hobbylobby.com)

HYGLOSS: Wholesaler and retailer of specialty paper and other crafting products. They carry self-adhesive velour paper, super-glossy paper, and metallic posterboard. (hygloss.com)

JO-ANN FABRIC AND CRAFTS: Fabric and crafting emporium throughout the U.S. (joann.com)

KNORR BEESWAX: Incredible deals on beeswax in a rainbow of colors. (knorrbeeswax.com)

M AND J TRIMMING: Known for their wide variety of trimming, ribbons, cording, lace, faux flowers, and more — an embellishing heaven. (mjtrim.com / 1-800-9-MJTRIM)

MICHAEL'S: Specialty retailer of arts and crafts materials with stores throughout U.S. and Canada. (michaels.com)

ORIENTAL TRADING CO.: Huge assortment of ready-to-embellish prefinished and unfinished wood products, scrapbooking and craft supplies. (orientaltrading.com)

WALMART: General craft supplies, faux flowers; many stores sell fabric and polar fleece, ribbons and trim by the yard. (walmart.com)

1-800-DREIDEL: Carries unusual Judaic-themed fabric and craft items such as matzo print fabric and shanah tova stamps. (1-800-dreidel.com)

ACKNOWLEDGMENTS A huge quantity of supplies was used for these projects. I am grateful for generous donations by **American Crafts** (americancrafts.com), **Cosmo Cricket** (cosmocricket.com), **EK Success** (eksuccess.com), **Heidi Swapp** (heidiswapp.com), **K and Company** (kandcompany.com), **Plaid** (plaidonline.com), **Provo Craft** (provocraft.com), **Tuvia's Judaica** (tuvia.com), and **Set Your Table** (845-371-7103). Special thanks to **Jackie Shafer** at Provo Craft for the ultimate die-cutting tools — the **Cricut** and **Cuttlebug** machines.

PARTY SUPPLIES Setting up for a party doesn't have to break the bank and take days of preparation. The following retailers are my go-to places for party goods; many of them kindly donated props for this book. Keep in mind, disposable dishes save the hassle of washing; or purchase inexpensive glass or ceramic plates and serving pieces that you can use over and over — another way to economize (just line someone up beforehand to help wash the dishes when the party is done!).

A PARTY SOURCE: Beautiful disposables, such as Yoshi square plates and china-look dishes, earth-friendly disposable bamboo dishes, and paper baking molds. (apartysource.com / 845-371-0220)

BED BATH AND BEYOND: Reasonably priced cloth napkins, serving pieces, glass dishes, bamboo place mats, table runners and chargers, and other goodies for the home. (bedbathandbeyond.com)

CRATE AND BARREL, and WILLIAMS-SONOMA: White earthenware dishes, ramekins, and serving pieces in all shapes and sizes, beautiful glassware and accessories. (crateandbarrel.com / williams-sonoma.com)

JAMAIL GARDEN SUPPLIES: A slew of garden accessories and floral supplies, as well as all sorts of props, vases, containers, and decorative accessories to make your party pop. 149 West 28th Street, NYC (jamailgarden.com)

KITCHEN CLIQUE: Huge selection of cookware and specialty bakeware as well as hard to find kosher ingredients. (kitchenclique.com)

MARSHALL'S, TJ MAXX, and HOMEGOODS: One-of-a-kind home fashions, including serving pieces, platters, cake stands, and tablecloths, at drastically reduced prices. (marshallsonline.com / tjmaxx.com / homegoods.com)

NER MITZVAH: Excellent source for plain and flower-shaped floating wicks and colorful Chanukah candles, tealights, and Shabbat candles. (nermitzvah.com)

OH NUTS!: Nuts, chocolates, and possibly every kosher candy available, sold either in bulk or in beautiful arrangements. (www.ohnuts.com)

PICK ON US: All sorts of party picks, skewers, and knotted bamboo skewers. (pickonus.com)

PLUM PARTY: Great party supplies for Chanukah and other occasions, and interesting items such as clown party picks. (plumparty.com)

TARGET: Expect great design on exclusive paper goods, plastic servingware, and funky party accessories at low prices — check out the "dollar spot" for great party goods. (target.com)

Index

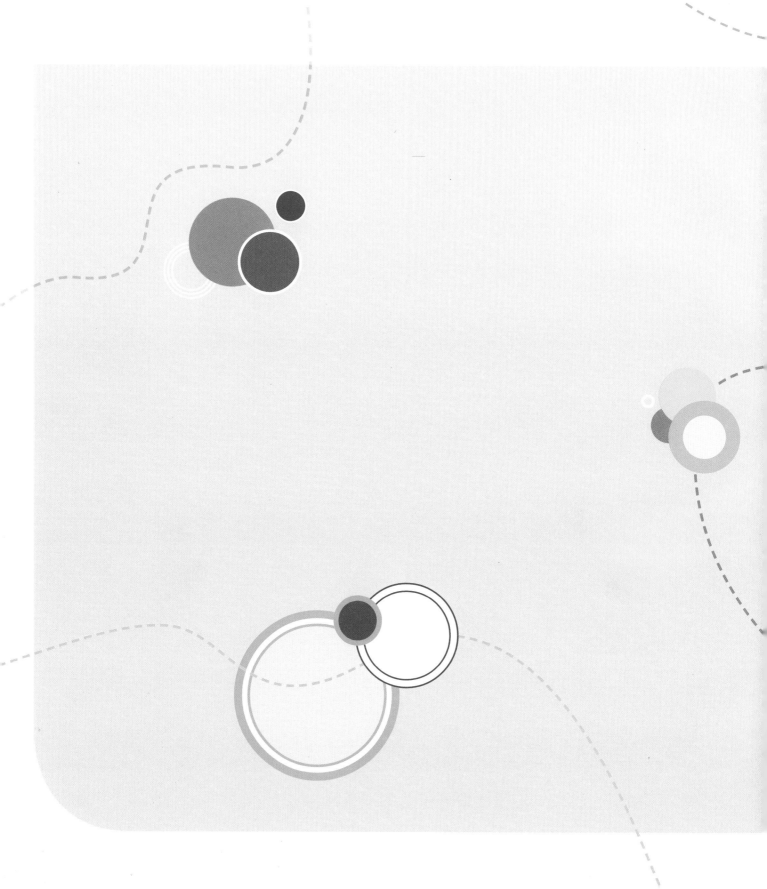